QUANTIFICATION IN HISTORY

QUANTIFICATION IN HISTORY

WILLIAM O. AYDELOTTE
University of Iowa

ADDISON-WESLEY PUBLISHING COMPANY
Reading, Massachusetts
Menlo Park, California · London · Don Mills, Ontario

This book is in the
ADDISON-WESLEY SERIES IN HISTORY

Consulting Editor
Robin W. Winks

Dedicated to M. K. A.

PROVENANCE OF THE ESSAYS, AND ACKNOWLEDGMENTS

Chapter 1, "Introduction," has not been published before. Chapter 2, "Quantification in History," to which I hold the copyright, originally appeared in the *American Historical Review*, **LXXI**, 3 (April, 1966), pages 803–825. Chapter 3, "The Problem of Historical Generalization," was first published under the title "Notes on the Problem of Historical Generalization" in Louis Gottschalk, ed., *Generalization in the Writing of History*: *A Report of the Committee on Historical Analysis of the Social Science Research Council* (Chicago and London, University of Chicago Press, 1963, © 1963 by the University of Chicago), pages 145–177. I acknowledge with thanks the permission of Professor Gottschalk and of the University of Chicago Press to republish the essay here.

Chapter 4, "A Data Archive for Modern British Political History," has not been published before. It will, however, appear in a volume of essays edited by Jacob M. Price and Val R. Lorwin which will be brought out by the Yale University Press later in 1971 with the title *Quantification and History*. This volume constitutes the proceedings of two conferences sponsored by the American Historical Association's Committee on Quantitative Data at Ann Arbor, Michigan, in November and December, 1967. The paper was written for and presented at the first of these conferences, and it was originally planned that it should appear first in the proceedings and then be republished in my own book of essays. The publication of the proceedings was, however, unexpectedly delayed, and it has been necessary to reverse this order. I wish to express my thanks to Professor Price and Professor Lorwin, and to the Yale University Press, for allowing me to go ahead with the publication of the essay here.

Chapter 5, "Problems of Method in a Particular Case: the Parliament of 1841," was previously issued under the title "A Statistical Analysis of the Parliament of 1841: Some Problems of Method," in the *Bulletin of the Institute of Historical Research*, **XXVII** (1954), pages 141–155. The present editor of the *Bulletin* has kindly given me permission to include it in this volume. Chapter 6, "Correspondence with Professor J. H. Hexter," has not appeared before. I wish to thank Professor Hexter for his cordial agreement to the publication of these letters. The three chapters that have been previously published, numbers 2, 3, and 5, are reprinted here as they originally appeared, with minor editorial revisions.

I am most grateful to the Graduate College of the University of Iowa for financial assistance which has made it possible for me to take time off to write.

I must also acknowledge a general debt to the many friends and colleagues, both in history and in related fields, in this country and abroad, who have read and commented on portions of this book or with whom I have discussed the topics it covers. Although I have profited enormously from their advice, the responsibility for the opinions expressed in these essays is, of course, mine only.

Iowa City, Iowa   W. O. A.
January 1971

CONTENTS

CHAPTER 1

INTRODUCTION

1 THE ARGUMENT OF THE BOOK

The papers in this volume are addressed to different facets of a single problem: how far quantitative or systematic methods can be useful in the study of history. This issue is raised, however, only in general terms. The book is not a technical manual; students who want help on the details of various research procedures should turn, as I have done for my own purposes, to other sources. These essays are principally directed to the broader and more rudimentary question of whether an approach of this kind is appropriate in history at all.

This is a question that, in the present state of historical thought and historical scholarship, still needs to be argued. It is curious that this should be so. The virtues of counting have been identified by occasional individuals for some years past, going back at least to Dr. Johnson.[1] The concern of historians with statistics is no recent development, but came surprisingly early. In the late nineteenth and early twentieth centuries a number of distinguished scholars, including Frederick Jackson Turner, A. Lawrence Lowell, and Charles A. Beard, showed an intelligent appreciation of the possibilities of quantification; and the work done by them and by their students foreshadowed some of the recent developments of historical study in several respects. The interest of American historians in such approaches died down, however, within the next couple of generations. The reasons for this are not entirely clear, though several plausible explanations have been conjectured: the inadequacy of the primitive statistical methods familiar to historians in the early twentieth century, and their lack of enterprise in searching for better ones; the growing availability of manuscript archives containing materials which, though of obvious interest and value, were not readily quantifiable; and the increased popularity of fields like diplomatic history or intellectual history in which there was less need for quantitative methods or, at least, in which the possibilities of applying them were less immediately apparent.

It is true that American historians have recently displayed a new interest in these methods. In the last several decades there have been published the results of a number of applications of quantitative techniques to historical problems, and the success and usefulness of some of these have been widely acknowledged. Interesting recent work along this line has been done elsewhere as well, for example in Great Britain and France. This revival, however, has taken place within only a limited segment of the profession. Some historians who deal with subjects for which these techniques would obviously be helpful show no inclination to use them. There seems to be a lack of understanding of the purposes these devices can serve and a lack of interest in the intellectual and logical problems with which they are designed to cope. Some extremely able recent writers have assumed a rather skeptical position in regard to the new methods. Anyone who thinks that this is a dead issue and that the battle about quantification is over should do some browsing in the bound volumes of *History and Theory*. There is obviously sharp disagreement on the subject. Questions have been raised about the value of quantitative methods, the importance and significance of the theoretical purposes for which they can be used, and the extent to which it is feasible to use them at all in dealing with historical materials and historical problems. It is clear that the matter still needs to be discussed and that answers to these three principal objections must be attempted.

I have tried to do this in the chapters that follow. The first point, the validity of quantitative methods, is discussed in Chapter 2. I have sought to indicate what is involved in the use of these techniques in historical research, what their advantages and disadvantages are, and what can be said in reply to some of the objections commonly made to them. The second question, regarding the theoretical purposes these methods can serve, the generalizations they can be used to test, is taken up in Chapter 3, where I have explored what kinds of general statements historians may reasonably attempt and have argued that, within certain limits, historical generalizations are both feasible and also highly desirable. The third question, the practical problems of using formal methods for historical materials, is treated in general terms in the second chapter and more specifically and concretely in the fourth and fifth chapters. I have tried to show that these problems, though they are great and should not be underestimated, are by no means insuperable. In the sixth section of the book, my correspondence with Professor Hexter, some of the questions that these approaches have raised in the minds of a number of thoughtful historians are aired and discussed. I have attempted, in my own letters, to show that these questions permit of acceptable answers.

In this introductory chapter I wish to explain somewhat more fully the structure of the argument of the book and how the various chapters are designed to fit into it and support it, and then to raise several general questions that underlie the whole discussion.

The second chapter, "Quantification in History," indicates the kind of value that quantitative methods can have for historical research and, at the same time, makes clear their limitations and the pitfalls that lie in the way of their use. I have no wish to peddle quantification as a patent medicine suitable to all cases and guaranteed to solve all problems. On the contrary, I have been cautious in my recommendation of it and I understand that I have come to be regarded, by some of the more advanced practitioners of the new methods in the profession, as a conservative. The position taken in this essay is that quantitative methods are applicable to only a limited number of historical questions, and that employing them when the evidence is inadequate or imprecise may, in effect, amount to nothing more than using the superficial trappings of systematic investigation to cover up loose thinking. On the other hand, quantitative techniques seem entirely feasible, within limits, for some kinds of historical research. They can, furthermore, be of great service when the evidence permits resort to them; and there seems reason to believe that a discriminating use of these methods can considerably facilitate the study of certain problems. I have arrived at the conviction that historians, in not taking greater advantage of quantitative techniques, have missed a major opportunity. They have unduly neglected a powerful instrument of analysis lying ready to hand and have neglected, also, rich materials to which this instrument would give them access and which it would enable them to exploit effectively.

The argument over quantification in history has, in considerable part, revolved around unreal issues. Some of the objections to it appear to arise, not from substantial intellectual differences, but from misconceptions about the purposes for which these techniques can be used or about the claims that can be made for them. No responsible practitioner of these methods would assert that all historical information can be quantified, that statistical tables provide any ultimate proof of the theories they are used to support, that the accuracy of the figures implies a similar accuracy of knowledge about the problem under examination, that quantitative procedures can achieve finality and eliminate subjective judgment, or that the adoption of these methods precludes the use of speculation, imagination, intuition, logic, and the other intellectual tools traditionally available for historians and for scholars in general. Claims of this kind are improper, and are not advanced by those informed on these matters. Among the skeptics, however, it is widely believed that such claims *are* made, that it is on such grounds that quantitative methods have been and must be defended, and that, in view of the inadequacy of these arguments, quantitative methods in history are unacceptable. Discussion of the subject has been hampered by the persistence of vulgar errors, and many of the objections that have been advanced are ill-informed or irrelevant. It is still necessary, in dealing with the matter, to steer one's way through a dreary tangle of clichés and stereotypes that have little to do with significant research problems. In the second essay, and also in the fifth, I have tried to clear away some of this debris, and to suggest what may be a more useful way of looking at these questions.

The third chapter, "The Problem of Historical Generalization," takes up the other side of the subject: not quantitative methods, but the theoretical uses to which they can be put. The chief value of these techniques for the historian is to verify generalizations, statements about several or a large number of instances. As has been pointed out in the second chapter, all generalizations are implicitly quantitative, whether or not this is made clear in presenting them; thus, those who attempt them must in some fashion have recourse to a quantitative approach. The need for generalizations in history, however, is another matter on which historians disagree. Professional resistance to quantification has been based, not only on a dislike of the method or a failure to understand it, but also on the larger ground that it is irrelevant to the main business of the historian, which is not to produce substantiated generalizations but to tell a story. This position has been asserted, skillfully and aggressively, by some of the ablest and most articulate historians and historical theorists of the present generation.

It is useless to try to lay down rules for the profession as a whole. Little can be gained by arguing in the abstract whether historians should generalize or tell stories. Historians do different things, and the test of the validity of what they do should be professional judgment of the results rather than the conformity of these results to a formula. Unquestionably some historians do attempt analytical work and do study problems the solution of which is likely to involve generalizations of some scope. To deny them the right to do this would be to impoverish the field. Others address themselves principally to narrative and description and, if their work is sound and proves useful, there is no reason why they should not. It is not necessary, for the purpose of the arguments in this book, to maintain that historians should make the production of verifiable generalizations their only task.

Strictly speaking, the matter is not quite so simple. I have suggested in the first section of the third chapter that the distinction between "facts" and "generalizations" is less easy to maintain than would appear from ordinary usage. There is a sense in which all historians generalize to some extent, and must if they are to speak intelligibly; any statement, to be understood, must be made in a context that implies one or several more general propositions. Discussion of whether historians should or should not generalize can, therefore, quickly bog down in an empty argument over nomenclature. I have tried to avoid this and to raise instead a question that seems to matter more: not *whether*, but *how far* historians should generalize, how broad they should try to make their statements, and how broad they can make them, while adhering to defensible standards of scholarship.

The position taken in the third chapter, that historians should and can attempt substantiated generalizations of some breadth, has been strenuously disputed. I have given the reasons for my views and have attempted to deal with the formidable arguments advanced on the other side. I have argued, I hope persuasively, that historical generalizations of a limited but still significant scope may properly be attempted; that, despite the complexity of historical materials, some headway can be made with the problem of verification; that the admittedly considerable difficulties of testing general statements do not warrant or excuse a surrender to impressionism or a failure to attempt such objectivity as is attainable; and that formal procedures are available for testing and supporting generalizations and for expressing the degree of their reliability with some precision.

The questions of verification, discussed in the second chapter, and of generalization, discussed in the third, are related, since presumably we should not try to produce generalizations for which we cannot make out some kind of case, and the scope of our generalizations will inevitably depend on the extent and quality of the evidence that can be mustered to support them. Though I have tried in the second essay to concentrate on problems of method, and in the third on problems of theory, these two matters are interdependent, neither can be discussed without considering the other, and it has been necessary to deal to some extent with both issues in each of the two chapters. Both essays were necessary to present a full statement of a position on the use of systematic methods of history.

This is still not enough, however. The case argued in the second and third chapters for testing historical generalizations by quantitative methods needs to be supplemented by a discussion of the third problem, the question of feasibility. Whatever may be the possible intellectual value of research of this kind, it still remains to be shown whether it can be done and whether the proposed avenues of exploration are, for practical purposes, actually open. It might indeed be contended that this issue is the crucial one. The objection is sometimes made that, while generalizations and quantitative methods may be fine in principle, historians forced to deal with disorderly and incomplete sources of information cannot attempt such tasks in any effective fashion. Doubts on this score are by no means without foundation, as will become apparent from the detailed discussion in the following chapters.

Some consideration of the concrete problems seems, therefore, essential: to ignore them would be to evade a necessary step in the argument. It is impossible to predict, on theoretical grounds, that research on a given topic will be possible. This becomes evident only when the problem is tackled and when the amount and quality of the available evidence are assessed. Unfortunately a good deal of what has been written on such matters has been precept rather than example.

It is easy to draw up a set of agenda for research, and many volunteers have shown themselves ready to undertake this agreeable task. To carry out the program, however, is a different matter, not only because of the work involved, but also because difficulties may develop along the way that were not foreseen or provided for in the original prospectus. One may justly regard with suspicion those who describe the task ahead but do not attempt it, who give persuasive advice but do not take it themselves. It sometimes seems as if the learned professions were divided into two groups, planners and doers, and that these two groups do not overlap as much as might be desired.

On this point I plead not guilty. Whatever may be the virtues or defects of my ideas about historical investigation, I have at least tried them out. I have entered the field of quantitative research not as an operator but as a practitioner, not as an entrepreneur but as a member of the proletariat. Some of my findings have been presented in a series of articles and papers, which are listed as an appendix to this book, and those who are skeptical of the procedures proposed here may wish to cast a sharp eye over these materials.

In the second chapter, I have argued in general terms that such approaches are feasible, within limits, in history and have given a number of examples of research projects in which they seem to have been effectively applied. The fourth and fifth chapters take up the issue of feasibility in more specific fashion. I cannot pretend to cover all aspects of so large a subject but can at least offer two papers that may go a limited distance to meet this legitimate question and to fill in this gap in the argument. These two essays approach the problem in different ways. The fourth chapter deals with assembling materials on a large scale and putting them into a form in which they can readily be made available to different scholars for a variety of purposes. The fifth chapter is concerned with some of the difficulties encountered in detailed research. Both deal with modern England, my own subject. If this seems unduly partisan, in a book addressed to a general reader, the reply must be that this is the one area in which I have studied the problems a little, and I can speak only of what I know. It is difficult to give concrete illustrations that are worth anything without drawing on one's own field of knowledge, and concrete illustrations are, for the reasons just explained, central to the argument. In any case, the fourth chapter does not deal at all with my own research while the fifth chapter, though it uses some of my findings for illustrative purposes, is principally addressed to more general questions.

It is a special, and unattractive, feature of quantitative research that it demands a lot of tiresome work. Gathering data is laborious and, for the most part, it is not a task that is intellectually challenging. It is true that some preliminary survey of the available materials is essential and that certain decisions must be made at an early stage as to what types of information will be most useful and are likely to be accessible, and also as to how these materials should be tabulated and arranged. These are indeed matters that require close attention. Once these plans have been worked out, however, there remains the long dreary routine of assembling the rest of the data according to these guidelines. This is a dull job and, though it must be done with care, it does not require great intellectual skill. It is also a more considerable task than will probably be realized by those not engaged in this type of work. The obligation resting on each scholar to collect his own materials has, in some cases, had the effect of limiting the scope of investigation: it is difficult for those who must do their own data-gathering to pursue interesting leads that may develop in the course of the project, after their money and their patience have run out. It can also happen—and this is particularly exasperating—that several students are interested in exploiting the same information, though perhaps for different purposes, and discover later that they have duplicated each other's work in a manner that was wasteful and unnecessary.

The existence of such problems has turned the attention of scholars to the possible value of large collections of the most basic kinds of data, which could be assembled and tabulated through a joint enterprise, put in machine-readable form, and made generally available. The attractiveness of data archives of this kind is that they can, in a measure, alter the character of the research: the student, instead of beginning with the uninviting work of tabulating his materials, can proceed more directly to tasks of analysis. The change is from an emphasis on semi-skilled labor to an emphasis on immediate confrontation with the intellectual problems. Several collections of this sort have been attempted for American political history, of which the most ambitious is the one that has been undertaken by the Inter-University Consortium for Political Research at Ann Arbor, Michigan. The program of the Consortium has now been carried some distance and has already provided materials on which American historians have drawn heavily during the last several years.

If this can be done for the United States, it may be possible to do it, or something like it, for other countries as well. The imposing effort of the Consortium offers a challenge to those interested in the political history of other areas. Comparable collections, if they could be made, would unquestionably be of great value. How far this can be accomplished is, however, a question to which we do not yet know the full answer. Although impressive starts have been made, both by individuals working alone and also by institutions or organizations, no enterprise on the scale of magnitude of the Consortium's project has yet been carried through elsewhere; nor, for most countries, have the possibilities been thoroughly examined and appraised. The question of feasibility cannot be answered in general or abstract terms. Political institutions differ from one nation to another and are not always easy to compare; and there are differences also in the extent and nature of the available evidence. It is necessary to consider in some detail the actual circumstances.

In the fourth chapter, "A Data Archive for Modern British Political History," I have attempted to make a contribution to the discussion by examining the possibility of collecting information, comparable to that being gathered by the Consortium, for Great Britain. I have tried to show how far this could be managed without doing violence to the evidence, to call attention to the principal difficulties and obstacles, and to identify the policy decisions that would have to be made. My position is that the gathering of at least certain classes of such materials for British political history in the nineteenth and twentieth centuries is entirely feasible. I have also introduced some remarks about the possible uses of such a collection of materials, particularly for the study of parliamentary history, which has been a subject of intense interest to British historians for the last couple of generations.

On the whole, this inquiry is limited to the collection of materials on lines parallel, so far as possible, to those laid down by the Consortium. It may happen, of course, that additional kinds of useful data could be obtained for other countries; and, when this is the case, consideration should be given to including them. Several such statistics have been discussed at the end of the first section of Chapter 4. They would not be difficult to get, and would be more illuminating for British than for

American history. Additions, however, should be introduced only when a fairly strong case can be made for them, since the duplication of the Consortium program for Great Britain, even with nothing added, would in itself be a considerable undertaking. Yet additions may properly be considered, by those who are willing to do the extra work, particularly if the experience now accumulated by the Consortium indicates that they are desirable. Subtractions from the Consortium scheme, the omission of categories that it is currently tabulating, on the other hand, unless the lack of information makes it impossible to include them, are open to objection, since they can be made only at the price of sacrificing comparability.

The question may be raised whether the Consortium scheme is the best one. Some students have felt that the county-level election figures it provides are not sufficiently detailed, that voting results on the township, ward, and precinct levels are also needed, and that certain problems can be properly studied only with the aid of materials based on these minor civil divisions. The question is not really that simple, for the addition of more detailed information is by no means precluded by the present guidelines of the Consortium, when financing can be obtained and when the data are available. The Consortium is not exclusively committed to county-level data and has already collected a certain amount of information for minor civil divisions as well. The optimum line of demarcation is not easy to settle. It is partly a matter of whether the more detailed evidence exists and is readily available, partly a matter of financing, for more refined classifications add greatly to the expense, and partly a matter of how much is lost by broader classifications or gained by narrower ones, which can be ascertained only by a certain amount of trial and error. I am certainly not competent to discuss this matter with regard to American history. Perhaps the point that should be made here is that policy questions that have been raised about the collection of American data should also be raised and considered in planning other data collections, and that every effort should be made to take advantage of the experience of the Consortium, much of which has been acquired the hard way, since it was a pioneer venture. The officers of the Consortium have certainly been most generous in placing their knowledge and the fruits of their experience at the disposal of others. In any case, whatever argument may arise over the details of the Consortium's plans, there can scarcely be two opinions about the general value of the materials it is collecting. These classes of information are central to the study of political history, and can serve the needs of scholars interested in a variety of different problems.

There is another reason for following the example of the Consortium, so far as is practicable and reasonable, in the collection of data for other countries: it would be a step in the direction of comparative studies in political history. The point is worth dwelling on for a moment since historians have not always shown themselves alert to the value of comparative research, and have been curiously unwilling to attempt parallel projects. New research enterprises are often not designed to test hypotheses already in the field. On the contrary, different historians tend to address themselves to different questions. The result is that their findings, though they may provide interesting general insights, are difficult to compare in any rigorous or exact fashion. The failure of historians studying similar subjects to ask quite the same questions of their data, or to gather the same kinds of data, has been a major obstacle to building a body of cumulative knowledge. Opportunities for checking the same points at different times and places have been missed. The determined individualism of historians in this respect seems difficult to justify, since it works against a desirable objective of scholarship and results in an impoverishment of knowledge. If historians were willing to investigate comparable problems by comparable means their efforts would be more effective, in that they would contribute to the development of a larger and more general picture. To deal effectively with general problems that transcend national boundaries it is essential that historians ask similar questions of similar materials so far as this is possible. Perhaps no two projects can be designed in exactly the same way, since circumstances differ from one research problem to another, but it seems reasonable to suppose that a great deal more could be done in the direction of agreeing upon common research objectives if historians were willing to take the trouble.

If students of the political history of different nations are going to study comparable classes of data, they must settle upon what these are to be. In reaching such a decision for other countries, the fact that a large collection of materials for the United States is already well advanced is hard to get around. To some extent the design of the Consortium's project imposes limitations on the design of similar projects for other countries. Even if were not an ideal scheme, one would be reluctant to change it without good reason since such changes would involve returning to the old state of anarchy, the old dilemma of trying to compare different political situations for which we do not have comparable information. In any case, the boundaries of the Consortium's scheme are not restrictive, and its general policy objectives are unquestionably defensible.

Whether there is any possibility that a project of the kind here suggested will actually be undertaken is another question. Certainly there has been much interest in Britain in quantitative research in political history, and some important work has already been done. Furthermore, British interest in data collecting on a large scale has been signalized by the establishment in 1967 of the British Data Bank at the University of Essex under the direction of Professor Allan Potter. As it happened, Professor Potter was present at the conference at which this paper was originally delivered and made a number of suggestions and comments for which I am most grateful. The British Data Bank is at present, I understand, principally concerned with the gathering of contemporary materials. There is, however, no reason in principle why its facilities could not be used for the collection or at least for the storage of historical information as well. I have no notion whether anything will ever come of my proposal for assembling data on modern British political history, and I am not presently involved in any scheme to implement the plan. I believe, however, that the plan is practicable, and I am concerned that it should be discussed and considered and that a fair case for it should be presented.

The fifth chapter, "Problems of Method in a Particular Case: The Parliament of 1841," deals in general terms with the advantages of quantitative methods and also with the difficulties of using them, and gives a few illustrations of both of these, particularly of the difficulties, drawn from my own work. The essay was written some time ago, when my research was at a different stage, and places more emphasis on matters of social analysis and taxonomy than on the subject with which I am most concerned at the moment, the study of votes. For this very reason, however, it helps to balance the book, particularly since it develops a number of points that should be covered but to which insufficient attention has been paid in the other chapters. The examples it gives of the practical problems I have had to face in my own investigations will help to show, in more concrete detail than could be given in the preceding chapters, the kinds of obstacles that appear when one gets into this line of work and, also, the kinds of solutions of these problems that can be attempted.

In the last section of the book, my correspondence with Professor J. H. Hexter, a number of questions regarding the implications of systematic methods for historical study, about which there has been a good deal of discussion, are raised and argued. The inclusion of private letters in a book of essays is an unusual procedure, yet Mr. Hexter and I both feel it can serve a useful purpose. A dialogue or direct confrontation of this kind can isolate issues and bring out disagreement about them more quickly and in some ways more sharply and effectively than would be possible in a formal presentation. The correspondence is an effort by two individuals who share certain assumptions, but do not see eye to eye on the lessons to be derived from them, to clarify their positions and to identify exactly what the points are on which they differ. The exchange may shed some light on the extent to which an attempt to use formal methods does or does not entail a break with the fundamental assumptions of historical investigation by more traditional means. The questions and reservations brought forward by Mr. Hexter with such address may have been present in the minds of others as well. I am happy to be able to include materials that ensure that both sides of the case will be presented, and I welcome the chance to argue these matters with a colleague whom I regard, even if I don't always agree with him, as one of the wisest and most perceptive of my friends in the profession.

2 THE CASE FOR FORMAL METHODS

I wish now to speak in broader terms about the purposes of this book and the concerns it represents. The essays presented here are in no sense designed as an all-out attack upon what are sometimes called, though the term is an oversimplification, the "traditional" methods of historical scholarship. Such a condemnation would be a sweeping, impressionistic judgment of the kind that I am principally concerned to argue against throughout the book. It would also be nonsense. Scholars of great talent have worked along what would now be described as traditional lines, and to jettison their achievements would be to deprive ourselves unnecessarily of a distinguished part of our intellectual heritage. It is even possible that, in this period of growing interest in new methods, the value of the kind of history that sets out to be narrative and description is sometimes underrated. Some proponents of quantitative methods come close to arguing that these methods constitute the sole means of obtaining reliable knowledge and that the fruits of scholarship in the prequantitative era may safely be disregarded. It is absurd, however, to contend that there is any exclusive road to knowledge, that intellectual rigor can be achieved only by the use of figures, or that the value of research depends on the kinds of techniques used rather than on the intelligence with which they are applied. Those who proclaim quantification as a new gospel of salvation, invalidating all earlier work, do the cause more harm than good.

Even so, responsible questions have been raised regarding certain approaches and practices in current historical scholarship of the traditional kind. These criticisms can, following the rough line of division used earlier, be grouped under two principal headings, the theoretical and the empirical aspects of research. They relate to the need for historians, on the one hand, to develop an adequate conceptual apparatus and to formulate general propositions systematically and, on the other hand, to verify these propositions by such means as are available, using quantitative tools if this can be done and if they are appropriate to the nature of the problem. It has been contended with some plausibility that, on both these points, the past performance of historians has not invariably been everything that could be desired.

The neglect of adequate theoretical analysis has been identified by a number of thoughtful members of the profession as a principal deficiency of modern historical study. The point is not that historians fail to generalize. On the contrary, many do so in a fairly uninhibited fashion. The stereotype that historians are interested only in the particular or the unique is not confirmed by their practice. The criticism is, rather, that historical generalizations tend to be unsystematic and unconsidered, that they are often introduced carelessly or incidentally, that their assumptions are not made explicit, and that their implications are not fully explored. Historians, it is argued, have on the whole paid insufficient attention to general problems of interpretation. In handling such questions they have displayed less care, less skill, and less imagination than they have shown in the performance of some of their other tasks. This deficiency may be due, as several writers have suggested, to the naive assumption, implicit in much of the so-called "scientific" history, that the data, once gathered and arranged in chronological order, would speak for themselves and that the conclusions would emerge directly from the evidence. The refusal, in much traditional historical writing, to explore theoretical questions and the implied denial that there were theoretical questions to be explored has in recent years been the subject of a good deal of comment. Arthur Schlesinger, Jr., who has not made himself known as a wholehearted advocate of the new methods, nevertheless feels free to admit "how dismally written history lacks in rigor, how impressionistic the historian's analysis so often is," and how great a need there is for historians "to criticize their assumptions, to expose their premises, [and] to tighten their logic . . ."[2] H. Stuart Hughes has objected to the "summary and unexamined" handling of the problem of causation by historians. Marc Bloch has contrasted the historian's scrupulous care in ascertaining whether an event had occurred with his amateurishness in offering an explanation of it.[3] R. G. Collingwood has described the legacy of positivism to modern historiography as an unprecedented mastery over small-scale problems combined with an unprecedented weakness in dealing with large-scale problems.[4] Lee Benson and Allan G. Bogue have commented on the theoretical inadequacy in much modern historical writing and on the reluctance of historians to take advantage of the more sophisticated theorizing in other disciplines from which they might derive useful leads.[5]

The failure of historians to give proper attention to major problems of interpretation has had unfortunate consequences which a number of observers have identified. Empirical research has been undertaken without adequate theoretical orientation, and without preliminary formulation of the most interesting questions to which the research might be addressed; as a result, labor has been wasted on problems that were intellectually trivial. Nor has the antitheoretical bent in historical study led to the exclusion of assumptions and theories from historical presentations. This, as David Potter has acutely pointed out, is scarcely possible since the historian must apply some theoretical assumptions to his data as the only alternative to leaving them in chaos. The result has rather, he suggests, been to incorporate into historical writing unexamined assumptions and theories. Potter argues that the habitual emphasis of historians on narrative and description has had the consequence that the majority of those trained in history have not faced or even identified important general questions with which they were inevitably concerned such as the nature of causation, of human motivation, or of social organization, and have tended to leave the systematic study of these subjects to workers in other fields.[6]

On the testing of general statements historians have also been found wanting. It is curious that this should be so. Over the last century and a half the problem of verification of assertions about the past has received intense attention from a long series of able scholars. Techniques have been worked out and standards set that, at their best, are impressive. The assessing of evidence has become, as Hexter says, one of the most treasured tricks in the trade. There is no need to disparage this revolution in research skills; it should, on the contrary, be regarded with respect. Yet a strong case can be made out that the development of the methods of historical research has been uneven. The high standards for verification that prevail in the profession have been applied principally to details. It is by no means clear that techniques of comparable rigor have been developed as far as they might be for the testing of more general statements. The question may fairly be raised whether all historians have taken full advantage of the means open to them for relating their generalizations to the empirical evidence at their disposal or, when such tests were not feasible, whether they have made fully clear to the reader the extent to which their general statements were speculations. Historians have seldom been able to avoid making general statements. They have in some cases, however, made them and handled them in a fashion that did not conform to the high standards of professional practice established for other aspects of historical presentation. All too often carefulness in checking details has been combined with fairly wild and impressionistic generalizations about the larger explanations that might account for them. Historians have produced a variety of intuitive insights which, though some of them may be penetrating and suggestive, do not always rest on secure ground. This procedure, however, is contrary to good research practice, in any field. History cannot be written as revelation. Bright ideas are not enough by themselves; it is also necessary to test them. Such insights, however attractive, are merely hypotheses, they are often of unequal value, and their worth cannot be determined until after a conscientious search has been made for all evidence that might tell for or against them.

Although the distinction between hypothesis and verification is fundamental to all research, it is not always appreciated or remembered. It sometimes happens that historians who work with the greatest strictness and probity in the handling of details will speak with more freedom and less strictness when they discuss larger matters on which evidence may be harder to come by. I have been particularly bothered by statements regarding the motivation of large groups of individuals since motivation, even for a single person, and still more for several, is an obscure subject, evidence on which it is usually difficult either to find or to interpret.

It would not, of course, be fair to describe the historical profession as a whole as lacking in insight into general theoretical problems or as irresponsible impressionists. The exact degree to which these criticisms are justified could be determined only on the basis of a more extended survey than need be under taken here. It is enough, for present purposes, to say that such practices appear to be sufficiently widespread to cause some restiveness among members of the profession and, in the opinion of a number of historians of the present generation, to constitute a problem. Certainly the impressionistic writing and the careless handling of general statements in some of the historical presentations of our own day has stimulated my own interest in techniques of verification and in formal methods of research. It has apparently also had this effect on others. I have discovered that my concern, far from being unique, is shared by a considerable and increasing group. Lee Benson has identified and described the problem in an eloquent and forceful statement and has, in his substantive work, made impressive strides toward a more formal and more tightly constructed type of historical analysis.[7] Allan Bogue, who has also been active in quantitative research, has described in his review article the increasing resort of a number of American historians to quantitative techniques and to systematic methods.[8]

We have heard something of the development of the so-called "behavioral" approach in political science, the increased interest of scholars in that field in obtaining results of greater empirical reliability and theoretical clarity. The movement has been characterized by Robert A. Dahl as one of protest: scholars who had become dissatisfied with the achievements of conventional political science attempted to work out methods and approaches that would provide theories of a systematic sort that could, in turn, be tested by close and rigorously controlled observation.[9] This reaction against earlier research procedures has, however, by no means been restricted to political scientists. The new lines of historical scholarship have been described by Bogue as arising out of a protest movement of a similar kind. They are at least partly due, he thinks, to a rebellion against certain weaknesses and limitations of conventional political history. Historians have sought for methods that would give them greater confidence in the results of research and for concepts that would provide a more satisfactory framework in which to present them.[10] The total volume of such work is not yet large and some of these studies are rather unsophisticated, technically and conceptually, when compared with those in other disciplines that have used such methods and have been concerned with such problems for a longer time. Nevertheless, the history profession, or a part of it, has been undergoing in the last several decades a sedate, hesitant, circumspect, little behavioral revolution of its own. The growing interest of historians in these new directions of research is attested by the organization of conferences and summer seminars, the training of graduate students, and of their teachers as well, in some of the requisite technical skills, the publication of articles, books, and collections of essays dealing with quantitative research, the establishment in 1962 of a standing committee of the American Historical Association which is concerned with quantitative data, the founding in 1967 of *The Historical Methods Newsletter*, the forthcoming publication of a text on quantitative methods for historians, and the circulation of a bibliographical guide.[11] The developments in history and in political science are presumably connected since historians have recently drawn increasingly upon political science, and upon the other social sciences as well, for both method and theory. The movement is a general one, and would appear to be gathering force.

It is still disputed, however, whether these approaches are likely to achieve the ends envisaged for them: greater theoretical refinement, and more adequate support of the conclusions of the argument. Some critics maintain that the hopes of practitioners of the new methods are illusory in both respects: that the emphasis on the technical aspects of research distracts the attention of students from theoretical matters and actually leads to a neglect of general problems of historical interpretation; and that, furthermore, it is absurd to suppose that historical statements can be tested with the rigor and precision to which the quantifiers pretend and, hence, their claim to have put the discussion of some historical questions on a firmer foundation of ordered knowledge cannot be accepted. These two objections, though much of what is said in the following chapters relates to them, are so central to the argument and have been so frequently advanced that they require some special attention at the outset.

The first of these criticisms is that quantitative techniques are, in their effective impact, antitheoretical since they result in an over-emphasis upon the mechanical aspects of research and a corresponding neglect of the intellectual tasks. According to this view, scholars who employ these methods are likely to direct their heaviest efforts to methodological refinements and the development of technical ex-pertise, and to show less interest in the implications of their findings for general problems of historical interpretation. They are also apt to select subjects for study that are technically manageable rather than theoretically important, and to pay insufficient attention to significant issues that may be difficult to handle statistically. This results in presentations that are arithmetically correct but intellectually trivial, that provide fairly reliable information on matters of no particular interest, and that are often, as well, carelessly or imperfectly thought through and badly written.

The most obvious answer to this criticism is that it entirely mis-takes the character of systematic research. The basic assumption of such research is that manipulations of the evidence are of little value unless guided by and tied to the development of a body of appropriate theory. This view, far from being denied or rejected by advocates of the new methods, has, on the contrary, been the cornerstone of their position. In research projects of this kind that have been successful, and that have influenced the thinking of the profession, the detailed empirical inquiry has been closely linked to the study of general problems of some scope and interest. Many students feel that the essential element in behavioral research is not quantitative techniques but analytical theory: that the significant impact of the behavioral revolution has been in theory rather than in method, in the new concepts that have been intro-duced and the new questions that have been raised rather than in the techniques that have been employed to investigate these matters. It has been suggested that discussions of the new methods and efforts to appraise them have often missed the point, in that they have been focused on incidentals rather than essentials, on means rather than ends, on methods rather than ideas. By this view, the employment of quantification in a mindless and purely empirical fashion is not systematic research but a caricature of it. It should be possible, then, to reply that the criticism is based on a complete misunderstanding of such research, and to dismiss it out of hand.

This is a good answer, but unfortunately it cannot be made. At least it cannot be made in a simple and unqualified form. The danger of concentrating on methods and neglecting the purposes they can serve does in fact exist, and it would be unrealistic to contend that it does not. This is one of the standard pitfalls against which beginners are customarily warned, but which they continue to fall into anyway. One can understand how this might happen. The adoption of a new method cannot in any case guarantee the possession of intelligence. Beyond this, students who have, with the best intentions, committed themselves to a high standard of exactness may hesitate to attempt important tasks which they fear they cannot handle with adequate precision. They may not even grasp these larger issues: a preoccupation with getting everything just right may make them unable to see beyond the ends of their noses. Dahl, who is certainly sympathetic to the new methods, has nevertheless expressed the concern that their impact may be to stimulate caution rather than boldness in the search for broad explanatory theories and that, as a result, empirical research may descend into trivialities. On the basis of my own experience I would agree with his diagnosis. In quantitative studies the danger of neglecting the theory has proved more considerable than the danger of neglecting the technical problems of handling the evidence. I have dealt with this point at greater length in the conclusion of the second chapter.

What this amounts to is that quantification needs to be defended from its friends as well as from its enemies. Not all historians who have tried their hands at these techniques have used them wisely or skillfully. Some have made elementary technical mistakes and have advanced claims for their results that were, simply on formal grounds, unallowable. This is bad enough, but at least it can be caught and corrected. A more serious problem, because it is more difficult to cope with, is that other students, while getting the technical parts right, have failed to meet the intellectual challenges and have not shown imagination in planning the tests they will make or in drawing inferences from the findings. All too often quantitative presentations, even when methodologically sound, turn out to be intellectually naive or pedestrian. Though the inadequacies of crude empiricism have been preached for years, an astonishing number of people continue to practice it or something close to it. Criticisms of the new methods on this point have some foundation in fact. The problem of having a technical mastery of the materials greater than one can keep up with in intellectual or theoretical terms, far from being unknown in quantitative research, might almost be described as the occupational disease of those who attempt this kind of work. It is widely acknowledged in conversation, if not in published statements. Lapses of this character have doubtless done something to discredit these methods and to arouse hostility to them which is directed, quite reasonably, against uses of them that should never have been attempted or against results that were not worth the trouble of obtaining.

It seems proper, then, in a book that makes a case for formal methods, to stress the importance of ideas. In systematic research, empirical and theoretical inquiry must be related and must proceed together; to neglect one at the expense of the other is to court disaster. The point was made earlier that is not enough to have ideas; one must also test them. The other side of this coin is that it is not enough to make tests; one must also have the ideas. Techniques are of little help unless due attention is given to the theoretical objectives for which they are employed and without which they are pointless. A student undertaking quantitative research should have a grasp of the intellectual context into which his enterprise fits and the possible bearing his findings may have on the general questions with which scholars are concerned. It is unwise to neglect any major possible path to this end. Here again a conservative note is appropriate. Though the new approaches are exciting and helpful, there is a danger of becoming so absorbed in them that one doesn't pay sufficient attention to what is good in the traditional methods of acquiring knowledge. It is possible that, in training students in new skills, older and more basic skills may be neglected. Indeed a student, even when he is committed to innovation, may find the earlier work in a field more helpful than he had expected. Much historical writing, even when it is not in the modern sense systematic and even when substantial revisions of its conclusions and its intellectual framework are in order, is nevertheless intelligent, rich in insights and ideas, and full of intellectual leads for someone alert enough to grasp them. A failure to take advantage of such resources, when they are available, may impoverish the quality of the final product.

The problem of inadequate attention to theory, however, though it exists and must be faced, can scarcely be attributed exclusively to the new methods. Nor have we any assurance that it would at once vanish if historians abandoned what some regard as the regrettable interest in technical innovation that they have displayed in the last several decades. On the contrary, such difficulties can appear in many different types of investigations. Any new tool can readily obtain a disproportionate share of the investigator's attention. This was a problem for the old history as well as for the new. The great reconstruction of research methods in history over the last century and a half was, after all, a revolution in technique rather than in theory. The essence of the "scientific" approach as conceived in the late ninteenth century was to get the facts, not to generalize about them. In an almost classic statement of this view Harold Temperley wrote: "But there remains a certain difference of emphasis between literary and scientific historians. The former tend primarily to generalizations and the latter to research."[12] Inadequate treatment of problems of theory and interpretation has been described as one of the outstanding weaknesses of traditional "scientific" history, and one that the new approaches were particularly designed to correct. It is ironical, then, that this charge should also be levelled against the new methods by the proponents of the old. Probably there is some justice in both accusations. This is a hazard in all intellectual enterprise. The technical side of research is usually easier than the thinking that should accompany it and, when this is the case, the techniques are likely to be emphasized at the expense of the ideas. The tendency to do this, to manipulate information rather than to think about it, is a disease from which we all suffer, a general human failing.

On this point, furthermore, a distinction can be made between the old and the new history with regard to intent. Whereas traditional historians have sometimes denied the need for theory altogether, practitioners of the new methods have recognized this need and tried to do something about it. They have attempted more rigorous definitions of terms and categories and of the problems to be investigated, and have made painstaking efforts to derive adequate explanations. Though they have not always succeeded in what they undertook, at least their conscious efforts have been pointed in this direction.

Nor have these efforts been uniformly unsuccessful. It cannot seriously be argued that all practitioners of systematic methods have been blind to the intellectual possibilities of their tasks. The more eminent men in the fields in which these methods are extensively used have recognized the danger of a single-minded emphasis on techniques and have taken pains to avoid it. Much of this work has been thoughtful, and the accumulation of new materials has been accompanied by the accumulation of new insights. In my own limited reading of this literature in other fields, I have actually benefited more from the insights than from the descriptions of techniques. These studies have been useful to me chiefly as sources of ideas that have put a different slant on some of my research problems, offered new and interesting perspectives, and disturbed my settled routine of thought. The new technical research in history has not been simply a matter of playing with figures. On the contrary, one of the most promising features of this development has been a conceptual one: a reappraisal and redefining of research objectives. Historians have not only been using new techniques but they have also begun to attack new problems that are of real interest and that have been identified in terms of radically changed intellectual schemes.

Finally, these remarks are not intended to leave the impression that an improvement in research skills is something that needs to be apologized for and explained away. To say that theory is central to this kind of work is not to deny the importance of trying to improve the technical apparatus as well. It is sometimes objected that talk about methodology is fighting in the air, that discussion of how to study history may simply divert scholars from the study of it, and that the way to make progress is to abandon the empty controversy over methods and to get down, instead, to concrete problems of research. I have given careful thought to this argument, and have concluded that it is specious. Doubtless observations about method have little value when they take the form merely of a pep-talk or of a statement of good intentions. The discussion of method can, however, amount to a good deal more than this. It can and should be a serious attempt to appraise various means of reaching firmer grounds for knowledge, considering both the advantages and the weaknesses of alternative instruments, what they can be expected to do and what they cannot, and perhaps trying them out experimentally or giving close attention to studies in which use has been made of them. Questions of this kind are not empty or trivial. An adequate examination of problems of method, if the matter is seriously pursued, should involve some thought about the basis of historical knowledge: it raises questions of what we know and what grounds we have for believing it, and forces a re-examination of the assumptions underlying our arguments and our research. A discussion of methods in this sense can be highly constructive, and students who wish to take full advantage of the various means open to them for dealing with their research problems can ill afford to ignore the subject.

The second ground on which it has been argued that quantitative methods are not likely to produce the results expected from them is that, except on a simplistic or trivial level, they cannot be effectively used for dealing with historical materials. The complexity of the historical record makes it impossible to handle all the relevant variables with the exactness that such an approach would necessitate. According to this view, the notion that historical investigations can be conducted and historical generalizations established with the precision and reliability that are attained in some of the more manageable disciplines, particularly in the natural sciences, rests on a complete misunderstanding of the nature of historical evidence. This evidence cannot, if the highest standards of modern research are adhered to, be made to yield universal laws, nor even general statements that hold without exception. Hence the claim of historians who use the new techniques, that they have placed general conclusions about major questions on a more reliable basis, is largely fraudulent, since the more significant problems of historical interpretation fall outside the reach of this net. It follows that the traditional emphasis in history upon narrative and description is sound and proper since it is based on a realistic appreciation of the limits of historical knowledge. Those who take this position admit that generalizations may sometimes be introduced in historical presentations, but insist that they play a subordinate role. General statements, it is argued, are designed to point up the narrative, to render its context intelligible, and to convey some of the insights of the writer, but are not intended to serve as the conclusions of the work. They represent judgments that, though not necessarily irresponsible, are looser and less clearly demonstrable than conclusions advanced in some of the stricter disciplines. In their formulation, imagination and intuition of necessity play a considerable role. General statements in history, by this view, should have and on the whole do have, as some historians have stated with almost embarrassing candor, an impressionistic basis.

This issue, the feasibility of making and testing general statements in history, is of course, extensively treated elsewhere in this book and there is no need to anticipate here the arguments that will be developed later. It may be useful, however, to say something about the frame of reference in which the problem can profitably be discussed. The position one takes on the issue of feasibility will obviously depend a good deal on the kind of general statement that is sought and expected, considered both in terms of its scope and also in terms of the degree of reliability that is claimed for it. On both these aspects of the question arguments have been advanced against formal methods in history that have beclouded the issue.

The point has been made, in the first place, that these methods have never produced, in the study of history or of politics and society in general, the universal laws that might be expected if these subjects were capable of being handled systematically. In replying to this argument it may at once be conceded that the laws of historical development produced by the system-builders—laws which, by the way, were usually not derived by quantitative means—have not met the test of professional criticism. They have, on the whole, been rejected by the profession on grounds that appear sound and reasonable and rest, as most experienced scholars would probably agree, on a mistaken notion of what can be done with historical materials. The absence of acceptable universal laws in history, however, scarcely demonstrates the impossibility of developing general statements in the field and testing them by systematic methods, even though it is used often enough as an argument to support this position. What is wrong with such an argument is that it pronounces against generalizations as a class without distinguishing between them in terms of their degree of generality. Yet, in deciding this question, the matter of scope is crucial. The argument that, since universal propositions cannot be produced in history, more limited ones cannot either, will not bear scrutiny. In the third chapter I have taken the position that it is absurd to suppose that all general statements in history need be of the "if, then always" type and that historians may most profitably address themselves not to universal laws, which are generally beyond their powers to handle, but to generalizations of a middle level in regard to which there is some hope of reaching reasonably secure ground and making a plausible case.

The other side of the argument designed to show that systematic methods in history are not feasible is that, not only have such methods signally failed to produce general laws, but also even limited generalizations reached by their aid are not wholly valid. This is because there are exceptions to almost all general statements. It is sometimes suggested, on this ground, that historians should refrain from making generalizations, that their business is rather to puncture the generalizations incautiously made by others and that, if they attempt generalizations themselves, they will be false to the high standards of accuracy set by modern historical scholarship.

This argument, though it is superficially plausible and though I have heard it advanced by reputable historians, actually distorts the question. It is true enough that there are likely to be exceptions to almost all generalizations of considerable scope that deal with a group of any size. In any extensive investigation it is virtually certain that not all the evidence will point in a single direction and that some of it will run counter to the most plausible theory or explanation that seems to emerge from the research. Yet the fact that almost all generalizations have exceptions, which is elementary, by no means implies that the quest for reliable general knowledge must be abandoned forthwith.

The point to make here is that means exist for dealing, on an intellectually respectable basis, with statements about a whole group that are only partially true. It is possible to handle these exceptions systematically. Figures can be used to show the drift of the evidence as a whole, to indicate how much of it tells for or against various alternative general propositions, and to state with exactness the degree of reliability of whatever conclusions are finally presented. In other words, quantitative methods provide a way to display the results of an inquiry without ambiguity, despite the ambiguous evidence on which they are almost always based, and to achieve precision in the face of uncertainty. It is easy, when one is describing a group all members of which have been observed, to deal in exact terms with a statement that is only partially true. One can say, for example, that, of the upper-class members of a legislature, 60 percent voted in favour of a given proposal while, of the lower-class members of the same legislature, 75 percent voted against it. This statement is perfectly adequate as a description of the evidence. It assumes, of course, that the social categories used are defensible and that the information on votes has been correctly tabulated. On these two points substantial and challenging questions may indeed arise. The problem of expressing a general statement to which there are exceptions is, by contrast, easy to resolve.

Furthermore this objection, if used as an argument against systematic methods, is singularly misdirected. The existence of exceptions to most generalizations is not a ground for avoiding quantitative techniques but an overwhelmingly strong reason for employing them. If most general statements have exceptions, then the objective in research that aims at conclusions of any scope should be to find out not whether these conclusions are wholly correct, which they presumably will not be, but how far they are correct. Quantitative procedures, when the evidence permits their use, afford the simplest and most effective way of ascertaining this. It is odd that such an argument should have been advanced against systematic methods and that there should be a widespread presumption, as there apparently is, that those who use such methods try to force everything into a single pattern and ignore the problem of exceptions. Quantifiers are, on the contrary, particularly alert to the existence of exceptions, of necessity, since their findings are almost never conclusive.

The remarks made so far apply chiefly to descriptive statistics, quantitative statements about a population all members of which have been observed. I have tried to show, in this chapter and the next, that even by these means much can be done in the way of overturning previously accepted opinions and establishing points that had not been properly understood before. This is partly, of course, because in many fields of history counting is still a novelty. Earlier writers have not always troubled to assemble their evidence in quantitative form, and many have injudiciously committed themselves to statements that were clearly wrong and that could easily have been set right by getting together a few figures.

Historians can also, however, resort to techniques of statistical inference and attempt to find out, from the study of a sample, something about the characteristics of the larger population from which the sample was drawn. Rather complex procedures have been worked out, and have now reached a high level of sophistication, for arriving at estimates, keyed to the conditions under which the sample was taken, of the degree of probability that the sample shares the attributes of the target population. These methods have been extensively used in survey research, the study of the attitudes of contemporary electorates, and have also proved themselves serviceable to historians in such areas as economic history and demographic history. For the most part, however, historians, so far as they have used quantitative techniques at all, have used only descriptive statistics, and fairly elementary methods at that. They have tended to shy away from problems involving inference and to confine themselves to the study of limited groups or limited classes of events, regarding which they hope to examine all of the evidence relevant to the questions they propound.

It may happen, however, that historians will in the course of time want to make more use of statistical inference. There can be no question about its value for problems on which the total evidence cannot be surveyed, either because it is too extensive or because a part of it has been lost. Often it is not profitable to gather all the available data on a subject. One may reach a point of diminishing returns, where additional evidence is not likely to alter the conclusions to an extent that would justify the effort spent in collecting it. In such cases it is better to sample, by methods as rigorous as the circumstances permit, and to use the available techniques and procedures to generalize from the sample to the original population. Cases also occur, only too frequently, when information on the whole group that is of interest to the historian cannot be had, when a substantial section of the evidence has disappeared and is now irretrievable. It is sometimes possible, in such instances, to consider circumstances which may have imparted a bias to the sample that remains, to take proper account of them and, by working along these lines, to produce some inferences, within a margin of error that can be stated, about the original population.

A formulation of research objectives in terms of a search for probabilities may be difficult for some historians to accept. Many in the profession, including some of those who use the new methods, still operate within an intellectual tradition that defines the purpose of investigation as trying to reach certain or final answers about the past. To them probable knowledge may seem inferior and unsatisfactory, not real knowledge; and the need to substitute probable statements for certain ones may appear humiliating. Such objections are, of course, wide of the mark. It is hard to find an acceptable logical ground for regarding statements of inference as an inferior form of knowledge. It is indeed argued that, with regard to matters on which the total evidence cannot be examined, we possess nothing but probable knowledge, and that this is true even in the natural sciences, as more accurate measures now show.[13] In our own age there has developed an increased appreciation and understanding of the importance of probable knowledge. This is doubtless largely due to the reformulation of statistical theory, and to its gradual penetration to a larger audience. Even within the field of history, however, the growing epistemological sophistication of those who discuss problems of historical interpretation has made it more possible for historians to accept a frame of reference of this kind.

Though historians may want definitive answers to large questions, they are not likely to get them, and they would do better to face this problem and to attack it in a systematic and organized fashion. This might seem at first like a retreat from the attempt to formulate strict laws of causation, but it can more properly be regarded as an advance. If historians seek to examine large problems on which they cannot survey the total evidence, the quest for finality is hopeless, and estimates of probabilities are the one kind of fairly reliable knowledge that they may expect to get. If they will recognize this, and address themselves to improving the quality of the estimates, they may find themselves operating in a more viable intellectual scheme that will enable them to move forward more rapidly.

Because of the possible eventual importance of statistical inference for historical research, it seemed desirable to say at least this much about it. A more extended discussion appears unnecessary, in view of the limited use made of it by historians at present. For most of the tasks historians set themselves these more refined tools are not required. This is true even when historical events are studied in a wider context, in terms of the general problems on which they may shed light. A historian, when he describes a limited group, may have at the back of his mind a larger population. He may see himself as making a contribution to the study of a more general problem that could be fully answered only by a series of similar investigations of comparable groups. Something of this may be implicit in any statement that attempts to be more than a description of a single event. Certainly it is highly desirable that historians should be alert to the broader implications of their work, since this gives more point and meaning to the research.

A consideration of these general matters need not, however, bring up problems of statistical inference. In fact it should not. A historian is not entitled to generalize to a larger population unless he can make a plausible case to show that the group he has studied is a properly selected random sample of it. Ordinarily, this cannot be done. It is quite possible for him, however, to report his findings in a wider context without going beyond his evidence. He can state that he has examined a major question, say the relation of political choice to personal background, in a particular situation, describe his results, and indicate the directions in which his evidence tends. If the relationships discovered are strong ones, and if they have theoretical implications of some interest, they are likely to be useful and suggestive to scholars interested in similar questions but working in other fields. The findings may indeed serve as the taking-off point for comparable studies designed to show how far the phenomena discovered were general ones or how far, on the contrary, they were restricted to a particular set of circumstances and did not recur.

Much of the attack against quantification has been based on the strategy of assigning to its advocates aspirations and claims that would not be accepted by any knowledgeable statistician and would at once be recognized as unrealistic by anyone with experience in historical research. The line of criticism discussed here, that quantitative generalizations in history are useless because they are not universal in scope and have exceptions, puts the whole question in a false light. It contrives to suggest that such methods, because they cannot accomplish the impossible, cannot accomplish anything. This would seem, at the least, to be a *non sequitur*. The fact that we are never likely to know the whole story does not mean that we can know nothing or that we must treat in slipshod fashion the little that we do know. The difficulties of deriving and verifying general statements in history may be conceded. I have expatiated on these difficulties at length in the chapters that follow and need say here only that I do not believe that I have underestimated them. If anything, I may have made too much of them.

My concern in recent years with problems of verification has brought home to me with increasing sharpness how little of what we want to say can be substantiated in a satisfactory fashion. The choice

in historical research, as in other research, is not between everything
or nothing but between better or worse. All knowledge is circum-
scribed, but this is not to say that it cannot be improved or that such
improvement is valueless. Even if historians cannot establish universal
laws, it does not follow from this that they cannot make some headway
with more limited propositions and place some of them on a more
secure foundation. They can, and have. Even if complete certainty
about general statements is unattainable, it does not follow that un-
restrained impressionism is the only alternative. Tests can be made and,
on some questions, it is possible to reach, if not finality, at least conclusions that we feel justified in putting forward with a certain amount
of assurance. It is naive to suppose that subjective elements in any
historical presentation can be entirely eliminated, but it is not naive to
believe that their role can be reduced. The admitted difficulties of
formulating and testing general statements in history are no excuse
for failing to make such efforts to overcome these difficulties as the
limited capacities of the human mind will allow. The object of quantitative methods in history, as of other methods, is not to produce the
ultimate at a moment's notice, but merely to carry us a little further
on our way. What it is reasonable to hope for is not the immediate
solution of major problems but, rather, findings that tell for one side
of a controverted issue or the other and make possible certain assertions about the subject that could not, before, have been put forward
with so much confidence. It has been well said that the difference
between an amateur and a professional, in their research presentations,
is that the amateur claims to have solved the problem while the professional claims only that he has found evidence bearing on it and pro-
ceeds to discuss what this bearing is, what may be inferred from it,
and how far it advances the argument.

The ultimate test of the feasibility of systematic research in history
must be an empirical one: whether it has actually been done and, if so,
whether it has produced results that seem reasonably convincing and
that are also of some theoretical interest. Certainly the amount of such
work that has been completed and published, though there is now a
fair amount of it, is only a tiny fraction of all the historical investigations that have been made. Quantitative research is still a relatively
new venture, and apparently most historians are still working along
nonquantitative lines. Also, what has been done varies in quality, as is

true of the work in most fields. On the other hand, it seems fair to say that there have been substantial advances, not in the sense of earth-shaking reformulations, but in the more modest sense indicated in the discussion above. Uniformities have been discovered and quantitative studies have thrown light on a variety of topics: the composition of various social or political groups, business history, agricultural history, roll-call votes in legislatures, patterns of voting in electorates, the social structure and the nature of social mobility, and a number of demographic and ecological questions. The results of these studies encourage the view that, within limits, these methods are quite feasible and that, in some cases, they can enable historians to move forward a good deal in making and testing general statements. The work done so far, as I have argued more fully in the next chapter, is of sufficient extent and of high enough quality so that allegations that it has produced no additions to knowledge and that it is inconsiderable or trivial cannot be seriously maintained.

It is possible that, by the ingenuity of scholars, the range of these techniques may be extended, and that they can be applied to an increasing number of subjects. It seems unwise to be overly pessimistic on this point since, more than once, there have been surprises: students have discovered how to use these methods to attack problems in ways that would not earlier have been expected. Some of the general issues raised in contemporary survey research are, for example, also being examined by historians to see whether it may be possible to study these basic questions about the nature of political behavior in the past as well as in the present. Some advances on this front have already been made. Clearly there are limits to what can be done. Not all historical questions can be answered simply by the application of more effective techniques. On important points the evidence may be elusive or unobtainable, and no technical apparatus can compensate for such deficiencies. Historians encounter considerable difficulties in the study of electorates since they must for the most part rely on aggregate data, with its attendant disadvantages, and they cannot even always get certain classes of aggregate data that they would much like to have. Unless there are special sources, such as the poll books kept at a number of British local parliamentary elections in the nineteenth century, it is hard to study members of the electorate individually. The sources for research on legislative bodies, on the other hand, often do permit the study of the actions of individuals in some detail and, by this means, make it possible to carry the analysis to a higher degree of refinement. My own view is that, for a historian, the study of legislative behavior is likely to be more rewarding than the study of electoral behavior. Not all historians are of this opinion, however, and certainly it has proved possible to do interesting work with electorates as well. In any case, decisions as to what can and cannot be investigated and what is worth investigating are a normal part of research strategy. It is seldom, in any field, that we can know all that we wish to know. It is necessary, in designing research, to play to strength, to select problems that are interesting in themselves, that can be treated with the materials at hand and, if possible, that relate to the points on which the evidence is most reliable and most abundant.

If the case were hopeless, of course, we should have to give up, but it obviously is not hopeless. It is sometimes said that political scientists, who work on contemporary problems and conduct polls and interviews, can observe political behavior directly whereas historians, who work in the past and cannot conduct interviews with the dead, are at a relative disadvantage. Certainly the sources that historians can use are often of a different character, and some avenues of investigation are barred to them. I am not sure, however, that the advantages are wholly on one side. Students of modern politics derive much of their information from written and printed materials that will be as available in a hundred years as they are today, and will presumably be at the disposal of historians in the future. Questions have been raised about the usefulness of interviews; self-ratings by respondents can be unreliable, and some political scientists within the last few years have been drawing attention to the limitations of interview techniques. Furthermore, a congressman or a member of parliament is likely to submit to only a limited total number of interviews, and some have been reported as displaying signs of restiveness. The historian, moreover, has some things working in his favor. His subjects are usually dead, so that there is no danger that the conduct of the inquiry or its findings will change their attitudes. This possibility is a real hazard in survey research. He has also the benefit of hindsight and knows what came of it all, which gives him a useful perspective and can suggest relevant questions to ask. He has much more extensive access to confidential materials than would be possible if he were studying a contemporary problem. Another advantage often overlooked is the fact that quantitative data for history, though not always the same as those available for the study of a contemporary problem, are abundant, particularly in the fields of economic, social, and political history. Man, as Paul Lazarsfeld has observed, is a data-producing animal. Furthermore, historical data are cheap. For the most part they need only to be taken out of books and records. Survey research is, by contrast, extremely expensive.

In the light of experience thus far, there seems no reason to suppose that an increased resort to quantitative methods will necessarily involve a descent into trivialities. On the contrary, the possible scope for such investigations has already been revealed as extremely broad. It is clear that rich materials are available. What is needed is the imagination to perceive their relevance to important problems and to organize them in such a way that they will shed light on these problems. The danger of triviality is more apt to arise, not from the lack of materials, but from the intellectual limitations of the scholars who exploit them. I have felt it necessary in this and in the following chapters to say a good deal about the difficulties of quantitative research in history and about the limits on what can be done. Perhaps I should make it clear that, despite these reservations, my own position is relatively optimistic; and I would argue that it is possible for historians to set their sights a good deal higher than they have.

It is central to the argument of this book that the value of quantitative research, as of any other research, is determined not by technical but by intellectual criteria. It depends, not upon the accuracy of the arithmetic or the complexity of the technical skills employed, but upon the interest of the problem studied and the intelligence that is brought to bear upon it. Nor does the success of the enterprise give an adequate indication of its importance. It may be of more value to advance a short distance on a major question than to provide overwhelmingly convincing support of a minor hypothesis that doesn't matter much one way or the other. Quantification is not a gimmick designed to solve all problems nor a universal specific. It is merely an ancillary tool, one of several, that can, for certain classes of questions, be of some help.

Some would put the case in stronger terms. It has been suggested that, for historians at least, quantification is a method so new and so revolutionary, both in the kinds of undertakings that it for the first time makes feasible and in the intellectual reformulations it entails, that it may be expected to inaugurate a new era of historical research. It should bring the study of human behavior in the past to a new level of exactitude, for the most part eliminate subjective factors in historical presentation, and for the first time make possible the study of history on a basis that might fairly be called scientific.

Though I am strong for the quantitative approach I think this line of argument, however well intentioned, goes too far, and oversells it. Such predictions, unless they are carefully spelled out and qualified, can be misleading. They claim too much and, indeed, claim the wrong things; to some extent they mistake the purpose of this approach and the kind of contribution it can make. I won't attempt to say whether history can be "scientific" since that word has been used in so many different senses that the discussion is likely to resolve itself into a question of definition. It seems more useful to consider, not this abstract question, but what specifically can or cannot be done. I do not, of course, propose to deny the advantages quantification can have for historical research. I have described it as merely an ancillary tool. This may seem to put it on a level with the typewriter or the fountain-pen, and in a way it is comparable to these. I would not, incidentally, disparage them either. Quantification is clearly, however, a tool of exceptional power, a considerable innovation in method, as innovations go, and perhaps "merely" is the wrong word to apply to it. It is a flexible and supple instrument that provides the means of doing urgently necessary jobs that could scarcely be attempted without it. For many historical problems it affords, not a way out, since that is not to be had in this life, but a means of getting considerably farther up the road. It has also opened up important new intellectual vistas; and the effective exploitation of quantitative techniques has, in the course of time, involved a significant amount of theoretical reorientation.

Yet I am not clear that all this involves a change of the fundamental objectives of historical research. We may ask new questions and we may be, with good reason, more ambitious regarding the range and accuracy of the conclusions we hope to reach. With the new methods, however, as with the old, we are still looking for explanatory statements about the past, though they may now be couched in different terms and may be, we hope, more persuasive and convincing. Nor can I agree with those who argue that quantitative methods will make possible final or certain answers to major historical questions. On some of these questions we can, by quantitative means, reach further into the issues involved and attain more secure ground in the answers we give. This security, however, is relative, not absolute. I consider predictions that finality of knowledge will emerge from a resort to numbers to be vain, for reasons that have been developed at length in the chapters that follow. Those who cherish such expectations can have had little experience with this kind of work. In any case, quantitative findings do not by themselves provide answers to general questions of interpretation. I have argued this again and again, but people don't seem to take it in. All that quantitative techniques can do is to re-arrange the evidence. The general conclusions of a quantitative study, on points that matter to us, are not proved by the figures. They are, rather, statements that have, we hope, some inherent plausibility and regarding which we can say that, after a conscientious search, we have not found a significantly large amount of evidence that tells against them. For this reason I hesitate to make so sharp a distinction between speculative statements and verified statements as some of the more ardent apologists for quantitative methods have done. Almost all statements are speculative to some extent, and it is undesirable to pretend to a degree of certainty that we are not likely to attain.

The notion that the historical profession is divided into two groups, quantifiers and nonquantifiers, is shallow and misleading, for it is not based on any important intellectual distinction. It arises, not from a major difference in research objectives, but from an intellectual time-lag. One might as well, to use again my earlier illustration, divide the profession into those who use typewriters and those who don't. There may be, for all I know to the contrary, interesting distinctions between typists and nontypists, but I would doubt that they loom large in the perspective of the main objectives of research.

Actually there is not in practice a great difference between a sophisticated traditionalist and a sophisticated quantifier. The former would admit the desirability of using all intellectual tools at our disposal, including counting and formal methods when they can help, and the need for avoiding slipshod thinking, though he would insist that the final interpretation of the results was a matter for judgment and argument. The quantifier would, if he knew his business, agree that the final interpretation of the results was a matter for judgment and argument, but would insist that formal methods have not been so extensively used as they might be and that there are many cases where more use of them would help the argument along. The intelligent traditionalist would concede the need for such objectivity as is attainable; the intelligent quantifier would concede that any pretense of having achieved complete objectivity is indefensible. The difference between a quantifier and a nonquantifier is not so great as the difference between a sensible man and a fool. Members of a department in making a new appointment do not, if they are wise, look for a quantifier but, rather, for a specialist in the desired subject, though they may also expect or even demand that, if he needs to use quantitative methods, he will be able to do so, or will learn how to. It is to be hoped that in the course of time quantifiers will come to be regarded as historians, if that is their field, and also that all historians will feel free to quantify when it suits their needs, and not to when it doesn't.

NOTES

1. See page 138.

2. Arthur M. Schlesinger, Jr., "The Humanist Looks at Empirical Social Research," *American Sociological Review*, **XXVII**, 6 (December, 1962), p. 768.

3. H. Stuart Hughes, "The Historian and the Social Scientist," *American Historical Review*, **LXVI,** 1 (October, 1960), pp. 24—25. Marc Bloch, *The Historian's Craft* (Eng. tr., New York, 1953), p. 195; cited by Hughes, p. 21. See page 90.

4. R. G. Collingwood, *The Idea of History* (Oxford, 1946), pp. 131—132.

5. Lee Benson, "Research Problems in American Political Historiography," in Mirra Komarovsky, ed., *Common Frontiers of the Social Sciences* (Glencoe, Illinois, 1957), pp. 113—183. Allan G. Bogue, "United States: The 'New' Political History," *Journal of Contemporary History*, **III,** 1 (January, 1968), pp. 5—27.

6. David M. Potter, "Explicit Data and Implicit Assumptions in Historical Study," in Louis Gottschalk, ed., *Generalization in the Writing of History: A Report of the Committee on Historical Analysis of the Social Science Research Council* (Chicago, 1963), pp. 178—179, 181.

7. Lee Benson: "Research Problems in American Political Historiography"; *The Concept of Jacksonian Democracy: New York as a Test Case* (Princeton,

1961); *Merchants, Farmers and Railroads: Railroad Regulation and New York Politics, 1850–1887* (Cambridge, Mass., 1955).

8. Bogue, "United States: The 'New' Political History," pp. 14 ff.

9. Robert A. Dahl, "The Behavioral Approach in Political Science: Epitaph for a Monument to a Successful Protest," *American Political Science Review,* **LV**, 4 (December, 1961), pp. 763–772.

10. Bogue, *Op. cit.,* pp. 19–22.

11. Robert P. Swierenga, ed., *Quantification in American History: Theory and Research* (New York, 1970), "Introduction," p. xii; "Clio and Computers: A Survey of Computerized Research in History," *Computers and the Humanities,* **5**, 1 (September, 1970), pp. 1–21. The book by Richard Jensen and Charles M. Dollar, *Quantitative Historical Research,* is in press in New York in 1970.

12. Harold Temperley, ed., *Selected Essays of J. B. Bury* (Cambridge, England, 1930), "Introduction," p. xxix.

13. Hans Reichenbach, *The Rise of Scientific Philosophy* (1951; 6th printing, Berkeley and Los Angeles, 1959), pp. 160–163.

CHAPTER 2

QUANTIFICATION IN HISTORY

Over the past generation a number of historians have recognized that
counting, when circumstances permit it, may assist in the study of a
limited class of historical problems. The historical monographs in
which quantitative methods have been used are already sufficiently
numerous so that a review of them would require an article by itself.
The purpose here is not to survey this literature but, instead, to raise
several general questions related to it. Professional opinion regarding
the value of quantification for history has been rather less than unani-
mous, and discussion of the subject has occasionally been acrimonious.
There have also been a few misunderstandings. I wish to consider what
is involved in trying to apply quantitative methods to history, what
kinds of results may be expected, and what difficulties lie in the way.
Though I shall say something about the advantages of quantification,
I am also, in a sense, concerned to speak against it and to make clear
the problems it presents. My own approach to the subject is conservative and skeptical, and at times I feel that the current fad for quantification has been pushed too far. In any case, the exploration of the
limitations of a method is an effective device for revealing its characteristic features.

The principal value of quantification for the study of history, stated
in the simplest terms, is that it provides a means of verifying general
statements. Some historians, of course, disclaim any intention of
making such statements and insist that the business of a historian is not
to generalize but to tell a story. Such a view can hardly be seriously
entertained as a description of the objectives of all historians, for it
manifestly does not apply to the work of a number of eminent members

39

of the profession. One might question, indeed, whether any historian can avoid generalizing altogether.[1] It is an idle task, however, to attempt a formal prescription of a historian's duties. If some wish to emphasize narrative more than others, there is no reason why they should not. History is what historians do, and they do different things. It would be presumptuous to dismiss any of their objectives as being in some fashion improper. The day of a single methodology in history, if it ever existed, is at any rate now gone. In a discipline where there are at present so much upheaval, reassessment of methods and values, and introduction of new approaches, it seems better to say that anything historians do is useful if it can be shown to be useful.

For historians who do wish to generalize, however, quantitative methods can offer certain advantages. Generalizations are implicitly quantitative in character, even though this may not always be clearly brought out. As Lee Benson says, historians who use words like "typical," "representative," "significant," "widespread," "growing," or "intense" are making quantitative statements whether or not they present figures to justify their assertions. Unfortunately, not all historians seem to realize the need to check general statements. Benson complains, in the same passage, of "the impressionistic approach long dominant in American historiography,"[2] and I have occasionally been bothered by this kind of thing in my own field. Historians justly pride themselves on their techniques of verification, which have become in some areas highly sophisticated. It seems fair to say, however, that these techniques have more often been applied to individual bits of information than to broader statements. Some writers, after a precise description of a few cases, will proceed to generalize blithely about the motives of large groups of men even though the evidence to support their views is often not presented and, indeed, would be hard to come by, for the motives of most men are obscure and not easy to discern. To an uncritical audience several concrete illustrations may carry more conviction than a statistical table. Yet to support an argument by only a few examples, though it may be a persuasive rhetorical device, is not logically adequate. There are exceptions to most historical generalizations, and, if the citation of occasional instances were accepted as proof, it would be possible to prove almost anything.

Quantitative methods, the numerical summary of comparable data, make it possible, in some cases, to avoid these pitfalls. The condensation of data by such means, when it is clearly legitimate, constitutes a saving of time and a convenience in that it makes the information easier to describe and to handle. It also helps to ensure a greater degree of accuracy. Memory is selective, and general impressions are notoriously untrustworthy. When the data are so numerous that they cannot all be kept clearly in mind at once, the investigator is likely to remember best the cases that fit his own preconceptions or his pet hypotheses. An orderly presentation of the evidence in quantitative form helps the student to escape the tricks that his memory plays upon him. Quantitative analyses are, of course, gratuitous when the number of cases is small, when the student is concerned with only a few men or, perhaps, one man, and when the general tenor of the materials can be immediately grasped. As the data become more numerous, however, a systematic arrangement of them becomes the more desirable. There are, indeed, some questions, of which examples will be given presently, which could hardly be attacked without the use of methods of this kind.

A quantitative presentation of the available information can help to direct the student's attention to the questions most worth investigating. Since it brings the whole of the evidence, on the point it covers, into intelligible focus, the general character of the findings can be more readily perceived and relationships and differences emerge that could not so easily have been observed without this reduction of the data. Such an analysis reveals what events or issues were of special interest, in the sense of involving change through time or departure from the norm, and hence might particularly repay investigation. It can, in this manner, help in defining or restating the historical problem to be studied.

Beyond this, a quantitative analysis offers a systematic means of testing hypotheses. It establishes how many examples there are to support each side of the argument and thus reveals not only the main features of the evidence but also, more important, the exceptions to them, the nuances, the degree to which the emerging generalizations need to be qualified. Measurement locates the defect in the original hypothesis and registers "the departure from theory with an authority and finesse that no qualitative technique can duplicate." A quantitative discrepancy between theory and observation is obtrusive. "No crisis is . . . so hard to suppress as one that derives from a quantitative anomaly that has resisted all the usual efforts at reconciliation."[3]

The general overview of the whole evidence obtained by quantitative means can also be a powerful stimulus toward the reformulation of one's ideas. When anomalies occur, the student can direct his attention to the cases that do not fit the original theory, try to find out why they are exceptional, and, by rearrangements of the data, test alternative hypotheses that may account for a larger proportion of the evidence. Such manipulations of the data would take an immense amount of time to do by hand, but, ordinarily, they can readily be performed by machines. I advise my students, if they are working with fifty cases or more, to punch the information. This is easily done, and once it is done, there is no great difficulty about trying additional correlations. By the same token a quantitative analysis can even, in some cases, point the way to the formulation of new hypotheses that will make the findings more intelligible.

The case for quantification might be made in still a different way by saying that it is a method of reasoning, one that involves number. As one of my colleagues at the University of Iowa has put it, quantification adds, to whatever factual or historical premises may have been established, the premises of mathematics as well. "Arithmetic is a vast treasure house of additional premises, or, what amounts to the same thing, of patterns of deductive inference. Quantification is the key to the treasure."[4]

The advantages of this approach have been appreciated by a number of present-day historians. G. Kitson Clark suggests as appropriate advice to someone who wishes to generalize about a group or a class: "do not guess, try to count, and if you cannot count, admit that you are guessing."[5] Lawrence Stone writes: "Owing to the obstinate perversity of human nature, it would no doubt be possible in England of 1958 to find, if one tried, declining manual labourers and rising landed gentry. To have any validity at all, conclusions about social movements must have a statistical basis."[6]

Applications of quantitative techniques to historical materials have, in some cases, materially advanced the discussion of major problems. Monographs on the composition of the British House of Commons, which are now fairly numerous and cover a span of six centuries, have brought to light significant continuities and changes in the social structure of the British political elite. Crane Brinton, in his well-known quantitative study of the members of the Jacobin Clubs, reached the conclusion that the Jacobins represented "a complete cross-section of their community" and that: "The Jacobins of 1794 were not a class, and their enemies the 'aristocrats' were not a class; the Terror was not chiefly then a phase of the class-struggle, but even more a civil war, a religious war."[7] Donald Greer, on the basis of a quantitative analysis of the victims of the Terror, argued that the lower classes, by the definitions he used, supplied 70 per cent of the victims and the upper classes less than 30 per cent and that: "The split in society was perpendicular, not horizontal. The Terror was an intra-class, not an inter-class, war."[8] From the researches of Brinton, Greer, and others, crude class theories about the French Revolution have received a set-back. Revisions have also been made in accepted views about American history. Richard P. McCormick published in the *American Historical Review* a set of tables, drawn from readily available election statistics, on the basis of which he was able to show that the great popular turn-out of 1824 was a myth and that: "In the 1824 election not a single one of the eighteen states in which the electors were chosen by popular vote attained the percentage of voter participation that had been reached before 1824." His finding contradicts the assertion he quotes from a standard text that, in the period before 1824, "only small numbers of citizens seem to have bothered to go to the polls." It contrasts also with Charles and Mary Beard's colorful statement that, by 1824, "the roaring flood of the new democracy was now foaming perilously near the crest . . ." and with Arthur M. Schlesinger, Jr.'s reference to the "immense popular vote" received by Jackson in 1824.[9] Albert Ludwig Kohlmeier, using statistical data on canal and riverboat traffic, was able to show when and how rapidly the trade of the Old Northwest shifted away from the South and to the Northeast.[10] Stephen Thernstrom, by a quantitative analysis based largely on census records, exploded various familiar hypotheses about social mobility in a Massachusetts town in the later nineteenth century.[11] Quantitative presentations have formed the basis for substantial generalizations by an impressive group of additional historians including Thomas B. Alexander, Bernard and Lotte Bailyn, Allan G. Bogue, Jean Delumeau, Robert W. Fogel, Frank L. Owsley, Lawrence Stone, Charles Tilly,

Sylvia L. Thrupp, and Sam B. Warner, Jr.[12] This list of examples could be considerably extended.

These results have often been achieved by fairly simple methods; for much historical research the quantitative procedures required are not complex. Historians do not ordinarily need to deal with problems of statistical inference in which an attempt is made to ascertain the characteristics of a large population by inspection of relatively small samples. Their work is usually limited to the easier task of descriptive statistics in which the object is to portray the characteristics of a group, all members of which have been studied, and to correlate some of these characteristics with each other. The computations needed for this are not ambitious. All that is generally required are a few totals, a few percentages, and a few correlations in which the relationship between certain variables is examined while other variables are controlled. This is a simple matter mathematically, although the research may be laborious, and it is simple mechanically as well. Even so modest a use of quantitative methods can sometimes produce results of great interest and can be used to test historical generalizations of some scope on which there has heretofore been scholarly disagreement. Since only a limited amount of such research has been done, much gold is still near the surface. It may turn out, however, that richer veins lie deeper. Though it has proved extremely useful to classify, arrange, and summarize the available information, it may be even more rewarding— to judge from some of the ventures that have already been made—to attempt more complex methods of descriptive statistical analysis by the use, for example, of mathematical models or of scaling techniques.[13]

Although substantial and interesting work has been done along these lines, much more could be attempted. Historians who have used quantitative methods have been timid in their application of them and have come nowhere near exploiting their full potentialities. Also, many historians who deal with problems for which such methods might be helpful have not tried to use them at all. Economic history is, perhaps, an exception. This field is naturally suited to quantitative research since many of the original data come in quantified form, the problems and hypotheses tend to assume a quantified shape, and, in the field of economics, theoretical analysis is more advanced. In political and social history, however, opportunities have been missed. Though the area of historical research to which these methods can be applied may be limited, it has certainly not yet been fully explored.

Furthermore, much hostility to quantitative methods still remains among some members of the historical profession. Despite what might seem the obvious advantages of these methods for certain kinds of problems, despite their notably successful application in many historical projects, and despite their long acceptance as a matter of course in several related disciplines, some historians still object to them vociferously and consider them altogether inappropriate for historical research. Questions have been raised regarding:

1. the quality of the work that has been done;
2. the feasibility of this approach in view of the admittedly limited materials available to historians;
3. the reliability of the results obtained by these techniques; and
4. the usefulness or significance of the results.

These objections are not wholly without foundation. It would be pointless to deny either the limitations of the method or the lapses of some of its practitioners. To concede this, however, is not to tell the whole story.

1. Certainly the ventures of historians into this kind of research have not been uniformly fortunate. Some of these studies, far from revolutionizing historical thought, have themselves not stood the test of time and have been shown to contain imperfections of method which, to some extent, vitiate their conclusions. It would be unfair to mention individual monographs without a more extended discussion of their arguments than is possible in this paper. I shall have occasion to describe some of the statistical solecisms committed by a few workers in my own field in separate articles on special topics. In general, it has been contended, sometimes plausibly, that a number of the pioneers in quantitative historical research overlooked certain elementary precautions. They did not, it is said, always appreciate or remember that a sample that is small and, hence, biased or unrepresentative may distort the results, that percentages should be figured in terms of what is hypothesized to be the independent variables, that a conscientious search should be made for all possible relevant variables (though it is unlikely that they can all be found), that failure to make such a search may produce spurious correlations, or that refinements of technique

cannot compensate for the inaccuracy or incompleteness of the original data. Doubtless the application of quantitative techniques to history has not paid off as well as might have been expected because of the statistical naïveté of a few of those who first tried it. To say this, however, is not to disparage quantitative methods. On the contrary, these are exactly the errors that an experienced statistician would not commit, and they arise not from an overemphasis but from an underemphasis on accepted statistical procedures. It may not be unreasonable to expect that simple technical errors of this kind will occur less frequently in the future as a new generation of historians becomes more alert to what is needed for this type of work.

2. A more serious objection is that quantitative techniques may not be feasible at all in history, or can be used only within narrow limits, because of the complexity of historical materials and the restrictions on historical knowledge. It is difficult to get accurate information, for the sources may prove inconsistent or unreliable. Also the task of correctly recording so great a mass of data is more arduous than is likely to be believed by anyone who has not tried it; the natural proclivity of almost all men to error, to incorrect observation, has been repeatedly shown by experiment. Beyond this, however, there are formidable problems of taxonomy. A given body of data can generally be classified in any of many different ways, and skill and experience are needed to choose the categories that will prove most useful. Unfortunately it may not become apparent which these are until one is well into the research and it is too late to change. It is also no easy matter to make the categories precise and clearly distinguishable from one another. The existing vocabulary of social history is inexact, and many of the terms in common usage are too vague to permit unequivocal classification of the data. To give one example, problems of this kind have, according to a recent review article, bedeviled research on the supposed conflict of the aristocracy and the bourgeoisie during the French Revolution. The ambiguities in the definitions of these terms have had the result that:

the central doctrine of the class struggle between bourgeois and aristocrats can now only be accepted as an act of faith; for no two people can agree on who the bourgeois and the aristocrats were; no one can formulate (and few even try to formulate) a criterion for distinguishing between them that can be followed consistently, and every argument is thus liable to be at variance with easily ascertainable facts.[14]

Similar problems arise, of course, in the social history of other countries. If a historian tries to distribute a group of men among conventional categories of this kind, borderline cases may necessitate so many subjective judgments that the resulting classifications will not be worth much. No amount of *expertise* in the manipulation of the figures will make adequate correction for imprecision in the original data or for categories that do not adequately measure what it is claimed that they measure. A quantitative approach does not of itself ensure accuracy. Jeremy Bentham's "felicific calculus" was set forth in quantitative terms, but it is not generally regarded as a precise conceptual scheme. There is a danger, in this kind of work, of a spurious precision—giving the results, to several decimal places, of calculations based on incorrect original assumptions. If the classifications used at the start are worthless, the computations based upon them will be equally so, no matter how many times they are passed through the computer, and the situation will develop which is known in the trade as "GIGO": "garbage in and garbage out."

Furthermore, historical information is restricted. Historians who seek to use quantitative methods are, in comparison to those working with contemporary affairs, at a disadvantage. It is difficult—and the difficulty generally increases with the remoteness of the period studied —to obtain relevant data for a large enough sample of the group or "population" under consideration to make a quantitative presentation useful and effective. It is feasible, for example, to study the composition of the British House of Commons in recent centuries, though the task becomes harder as one goes back in time, but it might be less rewarding to attempt an analysis of the personnel of Justinian's army.

Even some of the historians who have made conspicuously successful use of these methods complain frequently about the inadequacy of the sources with which they had to work. Brinton found the membership lists of the Jacobin Clubs incomplete, a problem heightened by the considerable turnover in membership, while the occupations of some Jacobins were not listed and the occupations of others were described in ambiguous terms. He insists that part of his information does not "have even the relative accuracy possible in a study of contemporary demography."[15] Greer speaks of "the impossibility of determining with any degree of exactitude the total death roll of the Terror."[16] Owsley found that the tax lists for many large areas of the South had not survived, while the census reports, besides being less accurate as a rule than the tax lists, were seriously incomplete except for the latter part of the *ante bellum* period.[17] Warner found rich statistical materials surviving for nineteenth-century Boston, but noted that city, state, and federal counts did not agree with each other and added the warning that: "The presence of substantial errors in the census requires the local historian to use census data with the same sophistication he would use any other source. The past tendency to check writings of individuals against other sources but to accept statistics as *prima facie* fact must be abandoned."[18]

Even in cases of groups for which quantitative methods can to some extent be used, it is not always possible to employ tests of sufficient refinement to verify what appear to be the most significant hypotheses. Benson, in his discussion of Beard's interpretation of the battle over the Constitution, has suggested that "we are likely to progress further if we group men, not according to their 'economic interests,'" but according to various other things including, for example, "their values, their beliefs, their symbols, their sense of identity."[19] Yet it may not be easy to obtain this kind of information for all or most members of a population of any size removed at some distance in time. It could, perhaps, be found for a few individuals on whom detailed information can be gathered from their correspondence and papers, but in statistics arguing from a few not necessarily representative examples is the great heresy. Doubtless more can be done than has always been realized, and, in another book, Benson has applied imagination and ingenuity to available materials to draw impressive and persuasive inferences on some of these difficult matters.[20] It can scarcely be denied, however, that these are obdurate questions, and anyone who tries to solve them has his work cut out for him; ingenuity can carry only a limited distance. For many groups in the past the kind of information needed to make such tests, much of it at least, has long since disappeared and is now irretrievable.

Clearly, formal statistical presentations are feasible only for a limited range of historical problems. The available information may be insufficient or may contain ambiguities that make it difficult to summarize in intelligible categories. Nothing is to be gained by pretending otherwise or by attempting to force the use of these methods beyond where evidence will carry. Frank Knight once observed that the dictum attributed to Lord Kelvin—"If you cannot measure, your knowledge is meagre and unsatisfactory"—has in practice been translated into the injunction: "If you cannot measure, measure anyhow."[21] This, of course, would be a counsel of darkness. Whether quantitative methods will be helpful on a given problem is a matter not of rule but of the strategy of research.

Though these difficulties are substantial, it would be a gross distortion to regard them as insuperable. Taxonomic problems vary in incidence, and it is mistaken to suppose that all subjects are equally difficult to quantify. Social categories may be tricky, but other kinds of information, such as votes in a legislative body, can be tabulated with some assurance. Economic and demographic data have been handled quantitatively with success for some time.

Even in the study of social history it has sometimes proved possible, as it has in scientific investigation,[22] to advance the argument by jettisoning subjective definitions and adopting objective ones, by disregarding earlier concepts that were too vaguely defined to admit of measurement, and by concentrating instead on categories that could be unmistakably specified—not "aristocrats," but peers and their sons; not "gentry," but men included by John Burke in his reference work *The Landed Gentry of Great Britain and Ireland*; not "businessmen," but men engaged in certain ways in certain types of business. Whether these more sharply defined categories correspond accurately to the old categories is a question that cannot be answered since the old ones are so indefinite that they cannot be said to correspond accurately to anything. One cannot, by using the new categories, effectively test propositions couched in terms of the old ones. Such propositions cannot, indeed, be tested at all, for an imprecise or slipshod formulation is impregnable; a statement that has no exact meaning cannot be disproved. What is feasible, however, is to study a group or an entity that might be conjectured to correspond somewhat to the old and loosely defined concept but that at least has the virtue that it can be identified. The investigator must, of course, assume the burden of showing that his new categories are viable and useful. The great step forward is to take the objective or unequivocal definition as the norm, as describing the entity that will be subjected to analysis, and to de- mote the subjective or vague concept to a subordinate position, to appreciate that, though it may serve as a useful starting point in the formulation of an operational definition, it may also contain variables that are difficult to measure or even to identify and that it cannot, there- fore, be handled in any conclusive fashion. By this procedure one at least knows where one stands, and the problems of social measurement may become less intractable.

Nor is the argument about limitations on historical knowledge really convincing. No doubt much valuable information has been lost. It is clear enough, however, that historical materials that lend them- selves to quantitative research, even if they do not cover everything, are enormously abundant. Some great storehouses of information such as census records and tax records are still relatively unused, except by a few pioneers. Other rich sources such as recorded votes in legislative bodies have been used only in a desultory and sporadic fashion, and much more could be done with them. Ample materials exist for col- lective biographies of groups of prominent individuals, and in some cases obscure ones too; for the economic and demographic character- ization of constituencies; and for ascertaining the relationship of the facts unearthed in such investigations to political choice.[23] Evidence is particularly rich for social and political history, two areas in which quantitative methods have not been extensively attempted.

Furthermore, it has proved possible, again and again, to describe in quantitative terms things that were formerly thought to fall beyond the reach of this net. Matters that seemed to an earlier generation un- quantifiable can sometimes be caught and measured by a change in approach or by reaching a clearer perspective concerning what it may be most profitable to measure. This applies, for example, to the study of attitudes, a field in which notable advances have been made over the last several decades. David Hume, speaking through the mouth of Philo, a man of "careless scepticism," argued that "controversies concerning the degrees of any quality or circumstance" can never "reach a reasonable certainty or precision." Thus, he says, it is im- possible to settle how great a general Hannibal was or "what epithet of praise Livy or Thucydides is entitled to . . . because the degrees of these qualities are not, like quantity or number, susceptible of any exact mensuration, which may be the standard in the controversy."[24] Even if we cannot measure qualities of excellence, however, we can perfectly well measure opinions about them, which are all we have to go on anyway, and this is done all the time with questionnaires. Similarly, ways have been found to measure degrees of liberalism and conservatism by indexes in which men have come to place some reliance, or degrees of attachment to a particular cause or principle, or degrees of interest or apathy regarding political questions, or even degrees of patient welfare in a hospital. It has been possible to do this last by a set of objective tests that fit into a cumulative scale and that have turned out to be reliable and consistent.[25]

Recent quantitative research in history contains several examples of a tour de force of this kind, attempts—fairly convincing attempts—to measure what previously seemed impossible to measure. One is the effort of Alfred H. Conrad and John R. Meyer to appraise the profitability of slavery and the efficiency of the slave labor market in the American South before the Civil War. It would be difficult to summarize here their complex and rather technical analysis, but it is interesting that their conclusions tell strongly against the long-standing though not wholly unchallenged view that the system of slavery was being underminded because of its unprofitability and because of the impossibility of maintaining and allocating a slave labor force. They found, on the contrary, that "slavery was apparently about as remunerative as alternative employments to which slave capital might have been put" and that: "Slavery was profitable to the whole South, the continuing demand for labor in the Cotton Belt ensuring returns to the breeding operation on the less productive land in the seaboard and border states."[26] Another example is the attempt by McCormick to describe, for the period in which he does research, the relation between the economic status of members of the electorate and their political choice. This topic, though important, is difficult for historians to study since the rich and poor in an electorate are generally buried in the anonymity of mass figures, and it is now virtually impossible to distinguish who voted for whom. McCormick, however, in attacking the problem, was able to take advantage of the dual franchise existing in North Carolina in the years 1836–1856, when only adult freemen who owned fifty acres of land within the county could vote for a member of the state senate while all freemen, including the above, who had paid county or state taxes, could vote for governor. By comparing, county by county, the size of the vote cast for governor with the comparable vote for state senators it was possible to determine the proportion of the electorate that could not meet the fifty-acre requirement. Then, by examining the distribution of each class of the electorate between the two major parties, McCormick was able to reach some conclusions on the relation of economic status to party affiliation. His finding, one of considerable interest, was that "the economic distinction implicit in the dual suffrage system had no substantial significance as a factor in determining party alignments in these North Carolina elections."[27]

In any case, the complexity and the limited scope of historical information are not arguments against quantification in particular. These limitations exist no matter what techniques are used. They arise from the insufficiency of the evidence and not from the peculiarities of the method. The obstacles to quantitative generalizations apply with equal force to nonquantitative ones, and what cannot be done with statistics cannot be done without them, either. No serious student of methodology would contend that a disciplined approach can overcome the inherent frailties in the data. But it hardly follows that, when the sources are suspect or the facts incomplete, an impressionistic, subjective approach can surmount these difficulties. Problems due to inadequacy of the data may be brought out more sharply and may become more apparent in a formal and systematic investigation, but they cannot in any circumstances be evaded.

3. The objection is also sometimes made that the general conclusions of a quantitative investigation are not proved by the figures. This is, of course, true, and no one who knows anything about statistical theory would argue otherwise. To expect finality for the broader conclusions of a quantitative investigation is to misconstrue the nature of the approach. On this point some misunderstanding apparently exists for, in everyday speech, reckless claims are sometimes made as to what "statistics prove." Actually the range of statistical proof is limited. A statistical table is nothing more than a convenient arrangement of the evidence and it proves only what it contains: that there was, for example, a relationship or, more usual, a partial relationship between two variables. Theories that attempt to account for such a relationship, in the sense of fitting the findings into a wider conceptual scheme, are

not proved by the figures. They are merely propositions that appear to explain what is known in a plausible fashion and that do not conflict with any relevant evidence that can, after a conscientious search, be uncovered. This is not to say that they are nonsense, for they may be supported by persuasive arguments. Yet since, notoriously, different arguments have proved persuasive to different audiences, the broader inferences from a quantitative investigation can scarcely be accepted as final. Thus it is possible, if the information is available, to establish how people voted, but it is much more difficult to say why they voted as they did. There might, of course, even be some difference of opinion on how they voted: for example, the accuracy of the records or of the tabulations made from them might be challenged. Yet such a disagreement is clearly on a lower level than a disagreement about men's motives, and there is a greater likelihood that it could be resolved through collecting and arranging the relevant data by acceptable procedures. In regard to more general explanatory propositions, however, a statistical inquiry, like any other method of verification, can only disprove. If the hypothesis does not fit the evidence, it may be rejected; in this sense a quantitative finding can indeed be conclusive. "Once we recognize that the Jacksonians won either by narrow majorities before 1837 or by narrow pluralities after that date, or frequently failed to win by any margin, it will surely become apparent that there is no basis for explanations that tell why they were the 'popular party.'"[28] The absence of unfavorable findings does not, however, prove an explanatory generalization for there may be some other explanation, and it is also possible that adverse evidence may be discovered later. Strictly speaking, a generalization of this kind is never proved and remains on probation indefinitely.[29]

Hence there is always, in quantitative research of any scope, a gap between observation and theory. To bridge this gap it may be necessary to resort to assumptions that are not demonstrated by the evidence. Some recent presentations of this kind depend not only on the figures but also on the use of hypotheses that are designed to show either what the figures measure or what their relevance is to certain general questions. The gap cannot always be bridged. Interesting findings may be obtained that are difficult to explain in the sense of devising an acceptable theory that will account for them. An example from my own research is a cumulative scale, derived through Louis Guttman's technique of scalogram analysis, that ties together votes in the House of

Commons on a number of different subjects in a way consistent with the hypothesis that they all measure a single variable. Yet the nature of this variable, this larger issue that subsumes many smaller ones, has proved difficult to determine. Though the existence of the scale can be demonstrated with about as much certainty as can ever be obtained in historical research, the characterization of it can be, for the present, only tentative and hypothetical.[30] Comparable dilemmas have sometimes been encountered in other fields.[31]

The hypotheses used to connect observation and theory are, no matter how plausible they at first appear, always open to challenge. The broader conclusions of a quantitative presentation may be vulnerable regardless of the accuracy of the mathematics or the reliability of the original data, and questions may be raised about them that cannot be answered by a resort to numbers. A critic may accept the findings, but then point out that the conclusions based upon them follow only if certain assumptions are made, and go on to question these assumptions. Some of the large modern quantitative studies have been criticized exactly on this ground: that the chain of argument, the series of connecting hypotheses, was too long and too tenuous to make the conclusions convincing.[32]

By the same token, a quantitative investigation may not and often will not settle an argument. It may settle certain disputed points about the evidence. The discussion of larger questions of historical interpretation, however, concerns not merely what the facts were but also what may be inferred from them, and on this level controversy may continue.[33] A quantitative finding may be open to more than one interpretation: in some cases it can be used to support either of two alternative and mutually exclusive theoretical schemes.[34] It can also happen that quantitative results that appear to disprove an accepted theory will simply be "explained away." This procedure can be quite legitimate, since it may prove possible to achieve a reformulation of the earlier view, which preserves some of the original insights, but does not conflict with the new evidence. If contradictory findings continue to accumulate, however, it may eventually be more satisfactory to abandon the earlier position altogether.

Quantitative procedures by no means preclude, nor indeed can they possibly eliminate, the use of value judgments, speculations, intelligent guesses, or "the imagination and intuitive feel which the historian, and for that matter the social scientist, should bring to his subject."[35] What is gained by attempting such exactitude as the circumstances allow is not finality but reasonable credibility, not the elimination of subjective factors but the minimizing of their role. No greater claim than this would be asserted by responsible social scientists or statisticians.

These points, though they are elementary, are not always understood or remembered. Quantitative findings are impressive in appearance and may, by their psychological impact, numb or blunt the critical abilities of the reader. It does occasionally seem to happen that a statistical presentation wins acceptance not through intellectual persuasion but through a kind of hypnosis. There is, however, no magic about quantitative evidence. It may be more conveniently arranged and, on the points it covers, more complete than other forms of documentation. Its significance, however, depends on what can be inferred from it, and such inferences, like all other inferences, may be fallible.

This disadvantage is not, of course, peculiar to quantitative procedures. On the contrary, quantitative evidence stands, in this respect, on a level with all other kinds of evidence, and arguing from it is subject to the same rules and the same hazards. The danger of false reasoning from good evidence occurs in any kind of research. It is not only in the field of statistics that men may agree on the facts but disagree on the inferences to be drawn from them.

4. Questions have been raised not merely regarding the feasibility and reliability of quantitative research in history but also regarding its usefulness. It is sometimes argued that quantitative findings, even if they can be trusted, tend to be trivial, inconsequential, and uninteresting. This is because any system of classification, such as is needed for such work, uses only a small part of the available information and leaves out the full richness of reality. Hence the ordinary statistical categories are too crude and threadbare to explain the complicated chains of events with which history is concerned. The problems in which historians are most interested are so complex that they elude these methods. One critic holds that: "almost all important questions are important precisely because they are not susceptible to quantitative answers."[36]

It is true, of course, that any quantitative procedure involves using only selected classes of data. It is seldom possible to include everything, or to come anywhere near this. Hence, statistical tables, though they seem impressive, may also present an appearance of bleakness or barrenness which can act as an impediment to thought. Often they will not stimulate the imagination as the detailed recital of an individual case will do. Indeed, it is useful, when one comes to an impasse in interpreting the figures, to turn to the consideration of individuals about whom much is known. Such individuals may not be representative, and one cannot generalize from them to the whole group; a study of them may, however, yield suggestions or leads, fresh hypotheses that can be tested, which will make the evidence as a whole more intelligible. It is always necessary, when working with the figures, to remember that they do not tell the whole story, that many elements of the situation are not reflected in them, and that what they do not cover may turn out to be more important than what they include. To interpret the quantitative evidence it is generally necessary to have recourse to the more conventional sources of historical information: memoirs and biographies, congressional debates, private papers, and the like.

The charge that quantification abstracts and uses only limited parts of the available information, however, is not an objection to this method specifically. On the contrary, any generalization abstracts. A generalization is a comparison of a number of cases, not in terms of all the attributes of each, but in terms of certain selected attributes in respect to which the cases are comparable. This problem is not peculiar to quantification; it arises in any research in which a conscientious effort is made to substantiate general statements.

The objection that the findings of quantitative studies are not significant sometimes takes other forms. It has been alleged, for example, that this kind of research is destructive and not constructive and that: "the recent use of quantitative methods to test historical generalization has resulted in the wholesale destruction of categories that previously held sway in the historian's vocabulary without supplanting them with new generalizations of comparable significance."[37] As an objection to quantification, however, this argument has no weight for it applies equally to any form of verification. All verification is in this sense negative. The argument fails to distinguish between the two quite different activities involved in research: getting ideas and testing them. Quantitative inquiries are generally directed to testing hypotheses formulated in advance. It has frequently been observed that, in work of this kind, a flat-footed empiricism is not likely to rise above a fairly low conceptual level and that systematic thought will progress more rapidly when it is directed by some adequate general hypothesis. The point should not be pushed too far for it occasionally happens that important relationships are not anticipated, but emerge as windfalls after the inquiry is completed. Also, in an area in which little work has been done, the original investigations must often be to some extent exploratory. It would be pedantic to insist on a full-fledged hypothesis in every case.[38] Nevertheless, the criticism that quantitative methods destroy and do not create is clearly based on a mistaken notion of the usual role of hypothesis in research. Hypotheses and generalizations are not simple inductions that emerge of their own accord from the evidence; they have, as is now better understood, different and more complex origins.[39]

Nor does a negative finding necessarily represent a dead end. If a generalization is wrong, it is useful to have it disproved; the disproof constitutes an advance in knowledge. As J. H. Hexter observes, "it may be worth saying that violent destruction is not necessarily of itself worthless and futile. Even though it leaves doubts about the right road for London, it helps if someone rips up, however violently, a 'To London' sign on the Dover cliffs pointing south."[40] A negative finding can be, in some cases, as valuable as a positive finding, depending on what theoretical inferences follow from it. Furthermore, to blame the quantitative method for disproving bad hypotheses is to blame the doctor instead of the disease. What is at fault is the mistaken opinion, not the technique that reveals when we have gone astray. The remedy is not to abandon the technique but to try to develop a new theory that fits the evidence better.

It is also sometimes argued that quantitative methods only prove the obvious, that they merely demonstrate, by an unnecessarily cumbersome apparatus, what everyone already knew.[41] It is admitted that they can occasionally be used to disprove certain crude generalizations that still appear in the textbooks. Yet, it is said, the crudity of such generalizations is already widely appreciated, and, on the whole, they are not accepted by sophisticated historians. In other words, quantitative techniques are useful only when historians have made fools of themselves. Their function is to clear away rubbish. However, if there is no rubbish, if scholarship in a field has been reasonably careful and responsible, a quantitative analysis is unlikely to reveal anything that is not already fairly well understood.

This criticism, also, is not well taken. Even if research merely confirms in a more conclusive fashion what some people already believe, it is good to have this additional assurance and to establish this belief on a more solid foundation. Also, on many questions that can be studied by quantitative methods, the answer is by no means a matter of course. More often there is evidence pointing in both directions, and both sides of the argument have been supported with some plausibility by different individuals. In such cases it is useful to establish which of two contradictory statements comes closer to describing the total evidence and just how close it comes. It might be added that, in disputes of this kind, either answer will be "obvious" in the sense of being already familiar, even though the two alternative answers exclude each other. Furthermore, the results of quantitative investigations have frequently told directly against interpretations that had been widely accepted. Several examples have already been given; another is Fogel's attempt to appraise the role of the railroads in American economic growth, which resulted in the conclusions, disheartening to some enthusiasts, that even in the absence of railroads the prairies would have been settled and exploited, that the combination of wagon and water transportation could have provided a relatively good substitute for the railroad, and that "no single innovation was vital for economic growth during the nineteenth century."[42]

Whether the results of a quantitative investigation are important or trivial is and can only be a matter of opinion. The presumption of significance is based not on a demonstration of fact but on a judgment of value. This applies, incidentally, even to the so-called "tests of significance" commonly used in statistics. Properly speaking, they are evaluations of probability, and, while probability can be mathematically determined, the degree of it that will be regarded as acceptable in any study is a question not of mathematics but of the investigator's preference. A quantitative study, it might be said, is significant if the investigator thinks it is and can persuade others to share his view. Speaking simply on this basis, it seems difficult to support the assertion that the topics open to quantitative investigation are of no consequence. Far from this being the case, an intelligent use of the method opens up a host of new, potentially interesting questions that could be approached in no other way. Some of these possibilities and some of the studies conducted along these lines have already been discussed. Perhaps it is enough to say here that the substantive weight of the findings of the limited number of historians who have attempted quantitative research is already impressive enough to render the accusation of triviality something less than plausible.

It seems reasonable to argue, furthermore, that the significance of a project of research does not depend on whether it is quantitative or not. Quantitative presentations vary greatly in value. They may be significant or trivial, interesting or uninteresting, and it is incorrect to suppose that they are all on the same level in these respects. What gives them such worth as they may have are the importance of the problem, the abundance, reliability, and relevance of the available evidence, and, above all, the intelligence with which the work is executed.

In fact, what is most needed in research of this kind is not the automatic application of certain techniques but, rather, qualities of logic and imagination. The main problems here, as in all research, are not technical and mechanical but intellectual and analytical. It is not easy to make the figures "talk" or to show their bearing on significant problems, and nothing is drearier than a presentation that merely summarizes the evidence. I am disturbed by students who want to do quantitative research and who seem to expect that this will solve their problems and that the application of a method will save them the trouble of thinking. This expectation is erroneous. Quantitative techniques, though they may play a crucial role in demolishing previous theories, are usually not adequate, by themselves, to establish general alternative hypotheses. They are nothing more than a means of deploying the evidence, although they perform this limited service wonderfully well. Once this subordinate and ancillary work has been done, however, the basic problems of historical interpretation still remain to be dealt with; they are not to be resolved by a gimmick. The greatest hazard in quantitative research is not that of neglecting techniques but that of becoming too much absorbed in them. This danger is particularly threatening now because of the rapid development of mechanical facilities for the processing of data. It is only too easy to become overly preoccupied with the gadgets and to forget the ideas. The refinement and sophistication of methods, though desirable in themselves, can become a kind of escapism, an evasion or postponement of the intellectual tasks that must ultimately be faced.

In general, the discussion of quantification in history has involved much talking at cross-purposes. Many of the common objections to this approach seem to arise from a misconception of its function. They appear to assume that claims have been made for it that no responsible statistician would make. No one well versed in this line of work would argue that all historical materials can be quantified, that the figures provide any final demonstration of the broader inferences derived from them, or that the figures tell the whole story. Such assertions are clearly improper. If they are not made, however, as by informed workers in this line they are not, much of the current offensive against quantitative techniques fails. The central point around which discussion of the subject has in part revolved is not an intellectual issue but a problem of communication.

The use of quantitative methods for history presents substantial difficulties not always appreciated by enthusiasts or neophytes. Those who have employed them are likely to be less starry-eyed about their possibilities than those who have merely commended them without trying them. Indeed, quantitative projects may be more glamorous in the planning stage than they are after the results have been gathered; the findings sometimes turn out to be flatter and less revolutionary than had been hoped.

Though the difficulties are real enough, however, it is not clear that they constitute objections specifically to a quantitative approach, or that they can be resolved by dispensing with it. The standard objections are misconceived or placed out of context when presented as grounds for rejecting these methods altogether. Properly understood, these reservations serve not to discredit quantification but to mark the boundaries of what it can accomplish. Indeed, the apparent disadvantages of quantitative research, the impediments to generalization that it presents, are actually advantages for they call attention to limits in knowledge or to flaws in reasoning that might not otherwise be perceived or fully appreciated. When all reservations have been made, quantification has still shown itself, in the light of the considerable experience we now have, to be a powerful tool in historical analysis. It helps to make the work both easier and more reliable, and, in some cases, it provides a means of dealing with questions that could not be attacked in any other way. Those wrestling with problems for which this approach is appropriate can ill afford to dispense with it. In the general intellectual twilight in which historians are condemned to spend their lives, even some small effort to render the darkness less opaque may be advantageous.

NOTES

1. The eleven contributors to a recent volume of essays on this subject, as the editor states in his summary: "all agree that the historian willy-nilly uses generalizations at different levels and of different kinds." (*Generalization in the Writing of History*, ed. Louis Gottschalk [Chicago, 1963], 208; see also, on this point, Alfred Cobban, *The Social Interpretation of the French Revolution* [Cambridge, Eng., 1964], pp.5–7.)

2. Lee Benson, "Research Problems in American Political Historiography," in *Common Frontiers of the Social Sciences*, ed. Mirra Komarovsky (Glencoe, Ill., 1957), p. 117.

3. Thomas S. Kuhn, "The Function of Measurement in Modern Physical Science," in *Quantification: A History of the Meaning of Measurement in the Natural and Social Sciences*, ed. Harry Woolf (Indianapolis, 1961), pp. 50, 52.

4. Gustav Bergmann, *Philosophy of Science* (Madison, Wis., 1957), p. 69.

5. G. Kitson Clark, *The Making of Victorian England* (London, 1962), p. 14.

6. Lawrence Stone, letter to editor, *Encounter*, **XI** (July 1958), p. 73.

7. Clarence Crane Brinton, *The Jacobins: An Essay in the New History* (New York, 1930), pp. 70–72.

8. Donald Greer, *The Incidence of the Terror during the French Revolution: A Statistical Interpretation* (Cambridge, Mass., 1935), pp. 97–98.

9. Richard P. McCormick, "New Perspectives on Jacksonian Politics," *American Historical Review*, LXV (Jan. 1960), pp. 288–301, esp. pp. 289–91; Richard Hofstadter *et al.*, *The American Republic* (2 vols., New York, 1959), **I**, p. 391; Charles A. and Mary R. Beard, *The Rise of American Civilization* (new ed., 2 vols., New York, 1931), **I**, p. 550; Arthur M. Schlesinger, Jr., *The Age of Jackson* (Boston, 1945), p. 36.

10. Albert Ludwig Kohlmeier, *The Old North-West as the Keystone of the Arch*

of American Federal Union: A Study in Commerce and Politics (Bloomington, Ind., 1938).

11. Stephan Thernstrom, *Poverty and Progress: Social Mobility in a Nineteenth Century City* (Cambridge, Mass., 1964).

12. Thomas B. Alexander *et al.*, "Who Were the Alabama Whigs?" *Alabama Review*, **XVI** (No. 1, 1963), pp. 5—19; Thomas B. Alexander and Peggy J. Duckworth, "Alabama Black Belt Whigs during Secession: A New Viewpoint," *ibid.*, **XVII** (No. 3, 1964), pp. 181—97; Bernard and Lotte Bailyn, *Massachusetts Shipping, 1697—1714: A Statistical Study* (Cambridge, Mass., 1959); Allan G. Bogue, *From Prairie to Corn Belt: Farming on the Illinois and Iowa Prairies in the Nineteenth Century* (Chicago, 1963); Jean Delumeau, *L'alun de Rome, xve—xixe siècle* (Paris, 1962), and *Le mouvement du port de Saint-Malo à la fin du xviie siècle, 1681—1700* (Rennes, 1962); Robert William Fogel, *Railroads and American Economic Growth: Essays in Econometric History* (Baltimore, 1964); Frank Lawrence Owsley, *Plain Folk of the Old South* (Baton Rouge, La., 1949); Lawrence Stone, "The Educational Revolution in England, 1560—1640," *Past and Present*, XXVIII (July 1964), pp. 41—80, and *The Crisis of the Aristocracy, 1558—1641* (Oxford, Eng., 1965); Charles Tilly, *The Vendée* (Cambridge, Mass., 1964); Sylvia L. Thrupp, *The Merchant Class of Medieval London, 1300—1500* (Chicago, 1948); Sam B. Warner, Jr., *Streetcar Suburbs: The Process of Growth in Boston, 1870—1900* (Cambridge, Mass., 1962).

13. On the use of models, see the review of the work of Harold Hotelling and others and the further discussion of this problem in Donald E. Stokes, "Spatial Models of Party Competition," *American Political Science Review*, **LVII** (June 1963), pp. 368—77. On scaling techniques, see Duncan MacRae, Jr., *Dimensions of Congressional Voting: A Statistical Study of the House of Representatives in the Eighty-first Congress* (Berkeley, Calif., 1958), and "Intraparty Divisions and Cabinet Coalitions in the Fourth French Republic," *Comparative Studies in Society and History,* **V** (Jan. 1963), pp. 164—211; William O. Aydelotte, "Voting Patterns in the British House of Commons in the 1840s," *ibid.*, 134—63.

14. Betty Behrens, " 'Straight History' and 'History in Depth': The Experience of Writers on Eighteenth-Century France," *Historical Journal*, **VIII** (No. 1, 1965), p. 125; see Greer's comments on the ambiguities of his own categories, in *Incidence of the Terror*, pp. 88—96; for a more extended discussion of these problems, see Cobban, *Social Interpretation of the French Revolution*, Chaps. III, VI, VIII—XIV.

15. Brinton, *Jacobins*, pp. 48—51, 57—58.

16. Greer, *Incidence of the Terror*, p. 37.

17. Owsley, *Plain Folk of the Old South*, pp. 150—51.

18. Warner, *Streetcar Suburbs*, pp. 173—74.

19. Lee Benson, *Turner and Beard: American Historical Writing Reconsidered* (Glencoe, Ill., 1960), pp. 169—70.

20. *Id., The Concept of Jacksonian Democracy: New York as a Test Case* (Princeton, N. J., 1961), Chaps. XII—XIV.

21. Kuhn, "Measurement," pp. 31, 34; remarks by Frank H. Knight in *Eleven Twenty-Six: A Decade of Social Science Research*, ed. Louis Wirth (Chicago, 1940), p. 169. The quotation ascribed to Kelvin appears on the façade of the Social Science Building at the University of Chicago. Kuhn has been unable to find these exact words in Kelvin's writings, though Kelvin expressed the idea more than once in slightly different language.

22. See the discussion of the development of the concept "degree of heat" in Kuhn, "Measurement," pp. 58—59.

23. An extended account of the work that has been done and that might be attempted along this line in American political history has been given by Samuel P. Hays in "New Possibilities for American Political History: The Social Analysis of Political Life," in *Sociology and History: Methods*, ed. Seymour Martin Lipset and Richard Hofstadter (New York, 1968), pp. 181—227; see also *idem.*, "Archival Sources for American Political History," *American Archivist*, **XXVIII** (Jan. 1965), pp. 17—30; and *idem.*, "Computers and Historical Research," in *Computers in Humanistic Research: Readings and Perspectives*, ed. Edmund A. Bowles (Englewood Cliffs, N.J., 1967), pp. 62—72.

24. David Hume, *Dialogues concerning Natural Religion* (London, 1779), Pt. XII.

25. Myrtle Kitchell Aydelotte, *An Investigation of the Relation between Nursing Activity and Patient Welfare* (Iowa City, Iowa, 1960), pp. 41—123.

26. Alfred H. Conrad and John R. Meyer, *The Economics of Slavery and Other Studies in Econometric History* (Chicago, 1964), pp. 66, 82.

27. Richard P. McCormick, "Suffrage Classes and Party Alignments: A Study in Voter Behavior," *Mississippi Valley Historical Review*, **XLVI** (Dec. 1959), pp. 398—403; for a review of other attempts to measure what cannot be measured directly and a discussion of the problems involved, see Robert William Fogel, "Reappraisals in American Economic History—Discussion," *American Economic Review*, **LIV** (May 1964), pp. 377—89.

28. Benson, *Concept of Jacksonian Democracy*, pp. 289—90.

29. For a further discussion of this point, see W. I. B. Beveridge, *The Art of Scientific Investigation* (rev. ed., New York, 1957), pp. 115–22.

30. Aydelotte, "Voting Patterns," pp. 148–51.

31. "In spite of the great social and scientific usefulness of psychological tests it must be acknowledged that for the most part we have had very inadequate ideas as to what it is that they actually measure." (Joy Paul Guilford, *Psychometric Methods* [2d ed., New York, 1954], p. 470.)

32. Nathan Glazer, " 'The American Soldier' as Science: Can Sociology Fulfil Its Ambitions?" *Commentary*, **VIII** (Nov. 1949), pp. 487–96; C. Wright Mills, *The Sociological Imagination* (New York, 1959), p. 72.

33. Greer based his conclusions on a calculation of what percentage each social or occupational group constituted of the total number of victims of the Terror. If he had argued from percentages figured in the other direction—designed to show what proportion of each of the various divisions of French society was executed in the Terror—the picture would have looked somewhat different. This is because, as Greer points out, the "proportional incidence" of the Terror was "almost directly inverse to its absolute incidence"; in proportion to their total numbers, "the nobles, the clergy, and the rich suffered far more than the lower classes." (Greer, *Incidence of the Terror*, pp. 105–109.) This aspect of the findings has been made the ground for a sharp critique of Greer's book by Richard Louie who argues that Greer's own data contradict his principal conclusion and show "with 95 per cent confidence that the Terror was an 'inter-class war.'" (Richard Louie, "The Incidence of the Terror: A Critique of a Statistical Interpretation," *French Historical Studies*, **III** [Spring 1964], pp. 379–89.) Neither way of presenting the figures is "right" in any ultimate sense; it is a matter of what question one wishes to answer and what features of the evidence it is most useful, for this purpose, to bring out.

34. In case this appears puzzling, it may be helpful to summarize the hypothetical illustration given by Hans Zeisel. If Company A increases its sales volume in a year from one to two million dollars and Company B, a bigger outfit to begin with, increases its sales in the same period from four to seven million dollars, then one could argue either that Company B did better since its net increase was three times that of A, or that Company A did better since it increased its sales 100 per cent in comparison to B's 75 per cent. Which alternative is preferred depends not on the figures but on what causal assumptions are implied in making the comparison and on what kinds of questions the investigator wishes to test. (Hans Zeisel, *Say It with Figures* [4th ed., New York, 1957], pp. 8–13.)

35. James Cornford, "The Transformation of Conservatism in the Late Nineteenth Century," *Victorian Studies*, **VII** (Sept. 1963), p. 40.

36. Arthur M. Schlesinger, Jr., "The Humanist Looks at Empirical Social Research," *American Sociological Review*, **XXVII** (Dec. 1962), p. 770.

37. Richard Hofstadter, "History and the Social Sciences," in *Varieties of History: From Voltaire to the Present*, ed. Fritz Stern (New York, 1956), pp. 415, n. 14.

38. Patricia L. Kendall and Paul F. Lazarsfeld, "Problems of Survey Analysis," in *Continuities in Social Research: Studies in the Scope and Method of "The American Soldier*," ed. Robert K. Merton and Paul F. Lazarsfeld (Glencoe, Ill., 1950), pp. 133, 137—42, 161; L. H. C. Tippett, *Statistics* (London, 1943), pp. 139—40.

39. I have discussed this point at greater length in Chapter 3 , pp. 83—92.

40. J. H. Hexter, "Storm over the Gentry," in *Reappraisals in History* (Evanston, Ill., 1961), p. 138.

41. Mills, *Sociological Imagination*, pp. 53—55, 75.

42. Fogel, *Railroads and American Economic Growth*, pp. 219, 234.

THE PROBLEM OF HISTORICAL GENERALIZATION

The problem of historical generalization is slippery and evasive. If historical generalizations are, as they are often said to be, qualified, tentative, and difficult to substantiate, these reservations also apply, with perhaps even greater force because of the second degree of removal, to generalizations about generalizations.

It seems especially presumptuous to try to prescribe for a field like history, since the practices and objectives of historians vary, and legitimately, with the field of study, the nature and quantity of the evidence available, the problems that seem important in a particular context, and the concerns and interests of individual historians. The subject has become to some extent a congeries of different disciplines, and one might hesitate to dismiss peremptorily any one of them as unimportant.

It is probably better, therefore, that anyone who discusses historical generalizations should speak so far as possible for his own experience. My interest is in quantified or statistical research, and it is this concern that I shall have chiefly in mind in the following remarks. The problems of statistical generalization, however, do not in essence differ from those involved in other kinds of generalizations—in a strict sense all generalizations are statistical, whether this is made explicit or not—and I hope that what I have to say about my own difficulties may bear on the problems of those who place a different emphasis in their research.

On the question of historical generalization some of the most acute modern historians have taken a very cautious position. Anyone who wishes to maintain, as I do, that such generalizations are both feasible and desirable must face impressive arguments that have been marshalled for the contrary opinion. Of these arguments I wish particularly to consider four:

1. That a "generalization" can take the form only of a general law, detachable from its context and applicable in all comparable situations and hence, because of the complexity of historical materials, entirely beyond the historian's grasp;

2. That no final proof can be given of any general statement because of the complexity of historical events, the limitations on the amount of information that can be recovered by the historian or digested by him, and the inescapable bias imposed either by the historian's own predilections or by the assumptions of the society in which he lives; that, since historical generalizations cannot be proved, historians who claim they can are merely deceiving themselves; that for these reasons no agreement can be achieved among historians about any general proposition; and that all generalizations, because of their inevitably flimsy character, should be relegated to a role wholly subordinate to the main business of the historian, which is telling a story based upon the facts;

3. That historians should address their chief efforts to insight and speculation, not to the hopeless objective of achieving demonstrable generalizations; that the best of their insights have been achieved and will be achieved not through labored documentation but through judgment, wisdom, and a maturity that comes only with experience; and that, therefore, such general statements as historians can make will be and should be personal, subjective, intuitive, speculative, and impressionistic; and

4. That, for these reasons, little can be gained from formal procedures, the hope that a recital of statistical evidence can take us deeper into the heart of reality is illusory, and the results of attempts to formulate general statements by these means have been trivial and inconsequential.

Though these four arguments are related they can be roughly distinguished for purposes of discussion. None of them can be lightly dismissed. The reservations they express serve in several ways to chart the limits of our knowledge. One may well wonder whether these difficulties are not so formidable as to deter historians from attempting to generalize in any extensive or ambitious fashion. My own view, however, is that this line has been rather overdone. My objection to these various points is not so much that they are unsound in themselves as that they have sometimes been pushed too far, into a context to which they do not apply, and have been made to yield inferences that do not necessarily follow. Reservations about the finality of historical knowledge are valid enough, but there is a danger of erecting them into a general law against any generalizations in history except on a subjective and intuitive plane. This forces the argument further than our experience warrants or than our practice assumes. It is in itself a generalization to which some of the above objections might legitimately be taken. I hope to show that this position is vulnerable at various points: that significant general statements need not be universal laws; that the problem of verification is not altogether insuperable; that intuition need not be the historian's final resort; and that effectual means exist whereby both the scope and the reliability of historical statements may be somewhat extended.

1 THE PROBLEM OF NOMENCLATURE

Disagreement about the feasibility of historical generalizations may rest, as many intellectual disputes do, on nothing more than an ambiguity in stating the problem. The dispute may be more one of theory than one of practice. Certainly some historians who express a formal skepticism about generalizations make them very briskly when they come to present their own findings. This scarcely settles the matter, however, for to show that a man's practice does not coincide with his theory is still not to answer his argument. The point is rather that historians who are optimistic and those who are pessimistic about the possibility of generalizing may simply be talking about different things: the optimists may be referring to contextual statements of limited scope, the pessimists to universal laws. Quite possibly the optimists and the pessimists would not differ greatly on the merits of a substantial number of historical propositions. Perhaps historians concur more on what kinds of statements they are prepared to make themselves or to accept from others than on how they describe these statements. If this is the case, the controversy over historical generalizations may be unreal, and the issue may have been played up beyond its actual importance.

If a "generalization" were defined as a general law, detachable from its context and applicable to all comparable situations and if this were adopted as an exclusive definition, it would have to be granted that historians do not often make generalizations and probably should not. Such a definition has occasionally been advanced. It has been said that a generalization must be an implication that holds true for all things of a certain kind, an "if, then always" statement, and that what we mean by explaining an observed fact is incorporating that fact into a general law.[1] By this view a generalization should be not a description of a finite set of cases which has no predictive claim but a statement about an unrestricted class of cases which comprises an "inductive leap" and which implies a prediction for all undescribed cases of the type that may ever exist, past, present, or future. Certainly the practice of most historians falls short of this. Historians, apart from the creators of the great historical systems, do not generally seek to formulate universally valid laws of historical development. Most historians restrict themselves to particular contexts and do not traffic much in universals, except perhaps for an occasional rhetorical flight.

It seems clear enough, however, in view of the many different senses in which the word *generalization* has been used, that to insist on the above definition as an exclusive one would be merely whimsical. The notion that a historical generalization can be only a statement of this character has been ably disputed by William Dray in his attack on what he calls the "covering-law theory."[2] Louis Gottschalk holds that it is sufficient to define a generalization merely as "a proposition that describes some attribute common to two or more objects."[3] David Riesman distinguishes between the "classic" approach aimed "primarily at generalizations that could in principle be true at any time and place" and the "romantic" approach which "is concerned with a particular people, in a particular time and place."[4] Others have sought to distinguish generalizations from other statements not in terms of scope but in terms of structure or purpose—by drawing lines that separate generalizations from trends, from hypotheses, from inferences, from classifications, and so on. The *Oxford English Dictionary* offers a string of definitions of *generalization* and *generalize* which, with the illustrations that accompany them, provide accommodation for almost every position that has been taken.

In view of these variations it seems unlikely that much would be gained by attempting a more refined definition of *generalization*. The word, like other key words, has in the course of time acquired a number of different meanings. The difficulties created by vagueness of usage cannot be escaped by elaborating a more precise vocabulary. To assign a single meaning to the term and to insist that all who did not use it in that sense were in the wrong would not only be arbitrary but would also render the ensuing argument highly vulnerable, since it could at once be rejected by all who did not accept the definition that it presupposed. An attempt at definition can become a kind of shadow-boxing that has little practical value.

If it is difficult to agree on what a generalization is, it may not be profitable to try to distinguish generalizations from other kinds of historical propositions. Doubtless a "generalization" is ordinarily conceived to be a statement broader than some other statement, but the term *broader* is relative. Putting it differently, one might say that all statements are generalizations but that some, those which we commonly and as a matter of convenience refer to by that designation, are broader than others. By this view, even the distinction between factual statements and generalizations is merely one of degree.

This point may be a stumbling block to many, for the distinction between facts and generalizations is widely accepted. A number of historians have insisted on the line between fact and theory, between particular and general statements, between statements that recite the data immediately observed and statements containing inferences and generalizations based upon them—between, for example, the information presented in a census return and the manipulation of this information to establish general propositions. Thus Sir Isaiah Berlin writes "The same facts can be arranged in many patterns, seen from many perspectives, displayed in many lights, all of them equally valid. . . . Yet through it all the facts themselves will remain relatively 'hard.'" He adds in a footnote: "Criteria of what is a fact or what constitutes empirical evidence are seldom in dispute within a given culture or profession." Berlin concedes that a boundary between facts and generalizations cannot be precisely established but regards this as of no importance. "We shall be reminded," he says, "that there is no sharp break between history and mythology; or history and metaphysics; and that in the same sense there is no sharp line between 'facts' and theories: that no absolute touchstone can in principle be produced; and this is true enough, but from it nothing startling follows. That these differences exist only metaphysicians have disputed."[5]

No doubt a distinction between generalizations and facts, even if it cannot be defended in strict argument, may still serve as a convenient short cut in referring to statements of greater or less complexity, and I shall occasionally employ it in this loose manner in these notes. Such a usage, though imprecise, is not wholly misleading: a difference in scope does matter and it is absurd to pretend otherwise or to regard the most simple and the most inclusive propositions as being on a par. The theory of natural selection is a generalization in a sense that the detailed findings of paleontology are not.

Yet the distinction between facts and generalizations has become increasingly unacceptable as historians have examined more explicitly and systematically their assumptions and their own mental processes. The difference seems one of degree rather than of kind and the line separating the two classes of statements, as even Berlin admits, must be arbitrary. "The distinction . . . between data and inferences," says Raymond Aron, "has a deceptive clarity. No one denies that in the most advanced natural sciences yesterday's inferences are today's givens. Propositions established mainly by means of inference become the data of which the scientist speaks. Theories and facts are integrated in such a manner that one would attempt in vain to separate them rigorously."[6] To argue as Berlin does that facts exist independently, as unchanging buildings blocks available for a variety of theoretical purposes, is to oversimplify. A "fact" cannot be apprehended or described by itself alone: a "factual" statement implies a predicate and cannot refer to something in an intellectual void with no points of reference around it. As Sidney Hook says: "Every fact which the historian establishes presupposes some theoretical construction." He adds: "There is only a difference of degree of generality and validity between facts and hypotheses and theories."[7] If what we commonly refer to as "facts" can be used as building blocks for a variety of purposes, so can low-level generalizations, and even high-level ones. The category of "generalizations" can include very simple statements, the category of "facts" very complex ones, and one would be at a loss where to draw the line between them.

It is better understood now than it used to be that the "facts" do not speak for themselves and that what we loosely refer to as factual statements turn out, when we consider them closely, to be based on an intricate chain of comparison, hypothesis, and verification, though these steps take place so rapidly that they are not always remembered or perceived. This applies even to our simplest observations, the "evidence of our own eyes." The point has been neatly illustrated by J. Z. Young in his account of experiments conducted on persons who, though born blind, were later operated on and received their sight.[8] The difficulty of training these individuals to interpret what the evidence of their own eyes actually was affords a striking example of what complex processes of deduction, inference, and speculation men go through when they perceive even the simplest "fact." The information gathered by a census-taker is sometimes cited in discussions of these problems as the simplest kind of raw data. Yet this information is recorded, and has little meaning unless it is so recorded, in categories which imply much previous thinking and generalizing. This may be why the techniques of census-taking have been greatly changed and improved over the last hundred years, as the basic assumptions that underlie them have been more clearly worked out.

The lack of any common agreement about what a generalization is and the ambiguity of the boundary separating generalizations from other statements are not, as Berlin suggests, trivial matters. On the contrary, they point the way to a reformulation of the problem. It follows from this line of argument that all historians generalize in that the statements they make cannot be distinguished from generalizations by any defensible criterion and that the claim made by some historians that they merely recite the evidence and permit the facts to speak for themselves is unallowable. Written history, like any other coherent or intelligible presentation, is not a simple record but something far more complex. Hence, the question whether historians should generalize or not is meaningless: they must generalize if they are to say anything worth saying. In this sense the controversy over the propriety of generalizing is indeed unreal, and it is pointless to argue about it.

In another sense, however, the problem is real enough. Variations in practice, in the kinds of generalizations historians have tried to make, indicate an extensive disagreement about what may properly be done with historical materials. This disagreement is no mere matter of semantics or of talking at cross purposes; it is concrete and substantial. General propositions offered by historians range in scope from the simplest to the most complex, from the narrowest to the most inclusive. Illustrations of the lower part of this range are scarcely needed. Since, however, it is sometimes said that historians habitually restrict themselves to "low-level" generalizations, cautious and limited statements of which they can be reasonably sure, it may be useful to cite a few illustrations drawn from the more rarefied upper part of the range which will show that this is by no means always the case:

1. "All the wars here discussed were preceded by a fall in prices on the London Stock Exchange and by a rise in the number of trade union members reported as unemployed."[9]
2. "The Speaker was a power in the House, but, as the Elizabethan period went on, his power was on the wane."[10]
3. "The prime minister replaced the sovereign as actual head of the executive when the choice of the prime minister no longer lay with the sovereign; the sovereign lost the choice when strongly organized, disciplined parliamentary parties came into existence; and party discipline depends primarily on the degree to which the member depends on the party for his seat."[11]
4. "A new Constitution does not produce its full effect as long as all its subjects were reared under an old Constitution, as long as its statesmen were trained by that old Constitution. It is not really tested till it comes to be worked by statesmen and among a people neither of whom are guided by a different experience."[12]
5. "All classes which have ever attained to dominion have earnestly endeavored to transmit to their descendants such political power as they have been able to acquire."[13]
6. "Modern technology created free society—but created it at the expense of the protective tissues which had bound together feudal society."[14]
7. "The man of the nineteenth century had a sense of *belonging* (deeper than mere optimism) that we lack."[15]

The first of these statements deals with a limited number of cases and is formulated in such a way that it could presumably be verified with some exactness. The second and third are broader in scope but still restricted to particular contexts. The fourth and fifth are couched in general terms and appear to be intended to apply to all cases of the type indicated. The sixth and seventh are contextual in that each purports to describe a single train of events, but are so sweeping that it might be difficult to verify them or perhaps even to say what they mean in any concrete or explicit sense.

It is in terms of this divergence in practice that the problem may be reformulated. It is pointless to ask whether historians should "generalize" if we cannot affix any distinguishing meaning to that word. It is not, however, pointless to ask how far historians should generalize: how broad or inclusive they can make their statements without departing too far from the standards customarily accepted for demonstration and verification. This question may not be easy to answer, the answers may be different for different kinds of historical enterprises, and perhaps no definitive answer can be given. The question is not meaningless, however. On the contrary, it seems to be the most profitable way of formulating the issue, and the rest of this article will deal with some of the points that should be raised if one is to take a position on it. The question of scope depends, in the first place, on the question of reliability. The problems of historical generalization and of historical proof are directly connected, and it is impossible to deal adequately with the first without considering the second.

2 THE PROBLEM OF PROOF

A major objection to historical generalizations is that they cannot be proved. By this view, which is certainly widely shared, it is naive to suppose that the evidence can be arranged in a clear pattern whose validity can be demonstrated, and attempts to do this rest on a misunderstanding of the kinds of materials with which historians must work and the kinds of problems they face. Robert R. Palmer, for example, agrees that a kind of wisdom gained from the study of one civilization "has some application to another (to deny this would condemn all history and social study to sterility), but I have no idea how this applicability can be stated with . . . rigor and precision. . . ." He says also, "Of any concrete and particular social and human situation, historical, currently political, or other, I doubt whether any significant generalization can be shown by evidence to be wholly valid or wholly invalid."[16] Chester G. Starr holds that generalizations cannot be verified, though facts can, and that historians may reach agreement about facts but do not at present possess the means of reaching agreement about general-izations. He is all for more generalizing, since to forego it would im-poverish historical literature, but he insists that it be done on an admittedly speculative basis.[17]

Criticisms of this kind have been directed particularly against the most daring generalizers of modern times, the builders of the great systems in history and the social sciences. Many of these systems were offered not as speculations but as "proved" sets of propositions: their authors claimed for them the precision and finality that they thought they observed in the natural sciences. Hobbes proposed to assimilate political theory to the state of perfection attained by the exact physi-cal sciences and claimed to be the Galileo of the science of politics. Gobineau spoke of "making history join the family of the natural sci-ences, of giving it . . . all the precision of this kind of knowledge," and described himself as the Copernicus of the historical world.[18] Henry Thomas Buckle hoped to accomplish for history something analogous to what had been effected for the natural sciences and to show how apparently capricious events were in accord with certain fixed and universal laws.[19] Toynbee maintains that the course of his-tory is governed by laws which can be empirically discovered and defined.

Though some of these schemes have great interest and represent impressive achievements both of learning and of systematic thought, they have on the whole been rejected, as adequate accounts of the his-torical process, by most historians today. The grounds for their rejec-tion have been much the same: that their claims to be empirical or "scientific" have not been made good, that they are not based upon the evidence, not in accord with the evidence, or not testable by the evi-dence. Toynbee's assertion that he has discovered general laws by empirical means has been vigorously disputed in a series of brilliant polemical articles by Pieter Geyl, who regards this claim as utterly unconvincing.[20] Professional opinion seems to incline toward Geyl's side rather than Toynbee's. All attempts to trace a structure of history, writes Isaiah Berlin,[21] "from the days of Herder and Saint-Simon, Hegel and Marx, to those of Spengler and Toynbee and their imita-tors," have been "always *a priori* for all protests to the contrary." General schemes of history have been notoriously vulnerable targets, and hardly any have withstood the test of critical examination over any long period of time. The disparity between the pretensions of the system-builders and the professional reception of their works might well serve as a caution against any effort to offer proof of general historical statements.

It is true, of course, that the reservations of historians toward these general schemes are by no means shared by many of those outside the profession. Geyl made a survey of reviews of Toynbee and found that those condemning him were mostly written by historians and those praising him mostly by nonhistorians. To historians Toynbee's work is unacceptable; to nonhistorians it is "an immortal masterpiece," "the greatest work of our time," and "probably the greatest historical work ever written."[22] Geyl will not allow Toynbee's claim that he reached his conclusions empirically; to Pitirim A. Sorokin, Toynbee's work displays "the technical competence of a meticulous empiricist."[23] The popular appeal of the systems, however, is, properly understood, no argument in their favor and no ground for disregarding our present reservations. This scarcely seems a case where the public is right and the experts are wrong. It is more probable that the uncritical acceptance of cosmologies by the lay public represents the desire, apparently implanted in most men, for an easy formula, a unified pattern in the confusion of life's experiences. Popular enthusiasm for these systems may not even reflect a historical judgment; it seems at times to have more of a religious or even superstitious character. As Perez Zagorin says, "Many people read Arnold J. Toynbee . . . as the Roman augurs read the flight of the birds."[24] Such enthusiasm, from an audience that does not comprehend the ingrained difficulties of the problem, is actually a ground for additional caution. The craving it reflects may appear within the profession as well as outside it, even if in a more sophisticated form, and a generalization may serve as a wish-fulfillment fantasy at a high intellectual level as well as at a low one. Perhaps historians have some reason to pride themselves on their resistance to this impulse and to pressures from outside their guild, and on the caution and objectivity which they have shown as a profession.

Certainly the impossibility of final proof of any historical generalization must be at once conceded. Our knowledge of the past is both too limited and too extensive. Only a minute fraction of what has happened has been recorded, and only too often the points on which we most need information are those on which our sources are most inadequate. On the other hand, the fragmentary and incomplete information we do have about the past is still far too abundant to prevent our coming readily to terms with it: its sheer bulk prevents its being easily manipulated, or even assimilated, for historical purposes. Further, historians deal with complex problems, and the pattern of the events they study, even supposing it to exist, seems too intricate to be easily grasped. Doubtless, finality of knowledge is impossible in all areas of study. We have learned through works of popularization how far this holds true even for the natural sciences, and, as Crane Brinton says, the historian no longer needs to feel that "the uncertainties and inaccuracies of his investigations leave him in a position of hopeless inferiority before the glorious certainties of physical science."[25] Nevertheless, these difficulties present themselves with greater weight in some fields than in others, and there is no use in deceiving ourselves by pretending the contrary. In history and other subjects that deal with the study of man in society they appear peculiarly intractable. The complexity of the historian's materials and problems, the number of variables he has to consider, the difficulty of isolating or successively eliminating these variables for purposes of inquiry, and the apparently unavoidable imprecision of his fundamental concepts, all serve to make his larger formulations difficult either to achieve or to defend.[26]

In addition, historians are fallible for reasons often beyond their control. Bert J. Loewenberg regards it as undeniable that "every intellectual effort is limited by the psychology of the person making it and the sociology of the conditions under which it is made."[27] A man's bias, personal concerns, interests, and proclivities may color, may impart a subjective distortion of which he is unaware not only to his selection of evidence but also to his notion of what constitutes proof. As Proust writes: "The facts of life do not penetrate to the sphere in which our beliefs are cherished . . . ; as it was not they that engendered these beliefs, so they are powerless to destroy them; they can aim at them continual blows of contradiction and disproof without weakening them." Arthur M. Schlesinger, Jr., quotes this statement to describe the soft-minded liberals of present-day America.[28] Yet there is no reason why it should not apply to others as well—Proust certainly couches his remark in general terms—and it is quite possible that those who pride themselves on being tough-minded may fall into the same trap. Certainly we can all recollect examples from our own experience of people who are willing to hold to beliefs despite the evidence or who derive what seem clearly mistaken conclusions from the facts before them. One thinks of Samuel Butler's anecdote of the man whose religious faith was restored by reading Burton's *Anatomy of Melancholy* because he thought he was reading Butler's *Analogy of Religion.*

A bias can also be cultural as well as personal. Even if a historian manages to identify his assumptions and his colleagues endeavor to correct his conclusions, the climate of opinion that surrounds them may impart a slant from which they can never fully emancipate themselves. Even the most carefully formulated statements may be *zeitgebunden* in ways that contemporaries will not perceive.

It must be remembered that "proof" is not something external to the human mind. The validity of a historical statement depends not simply on the arguments and evidence adduced in its support but on the acceptance of these arguments and evidence by one or more individuals, presumably those competent to judge. Further, since men's judgments of their own work are notoriously liable to error, the approval of others has come to be accepted as the sounder, though not necessarily infallible, test. By this view a generalization is valid to the extent that it is communicable or acceptable to others, and the historian (or anyone else) ultimately rests his case not on logic but on persuasion, though the former may be a means toward the latter. If, however, we have no better test of "proof" than consensus, the possibilities of finality seem to be rather remote. Professional opinion may be fragmented, so that the consensus is not clear. When there is general agreement, matters may actually be worse, for the consensus of professional opinion has often proved mistaken and has, further, often been singularly unwilling to approve new ideas upon their first appearance. Sir Lewis Namier has written that a new historical interpretation should, once it is formulated, appear so obvious as to command instant acceptance; this did not happen, however, in the case of his own considerable innovations, which were not appreciated in anything like their full significance until some years after their publication. Intellectual history is full of instances where contemporaries failed to understand the value or even the meaning of some of the most impor-

tant intellectual enterprises of their own day. Some works were slight-
ed for reasons that later proved irrelevant; others were for a time estimated more highly than we now think they deserved. Nor is it always
clear whose consensus is wanted. It would hardly do to say that the
validity of a statement should be measured on the simple democratic
basis of the number of its adherents. Such a principle would at once
reinstate Toynbee and throw his critics out of court. A historian seeks
to convince not all men but a learned audience, whose boundaries
nevertheless cannot be very clearly discerned. A criterion of consensus
can also, and perhaps often does, lead to a debasing of the historical
craft: a historian may become "other-directed" and say not what he
himself believes or considers most important but what he thinks will
appeal to his audience; or, again, he may become a kind of sophist,
concentrating not on the art of discovery but on the techniques of
persuasion.

These ambiguities are well understood today and historians seem
highly alert to the complexity and evasiveness of historical problems.
Hans Meyerhoff, in a note in his recent anthology on the philosophy of
history, comments on the fact that the philosophers whose essays he
includes "are primarily concerned with defending the possibility of
an objective history," whereas the historians who join the debate "are
conscious, to different degrees, of the ineluctably subjective factors
... that seem to intrude upon the subject of history."[29] Geyl finds
modern historians overcautious rather than overbold: "This much is
certain: the quality which the academic and specialized study of history tends to develop is that of caution.... The prevailing mood
among professional historians nowadays is a chastened one in the face
of the immense mass of material and the infinite complexity of the
phenomena."[30] Perhaps many contemporary historians would agree
that they spend their time in an atmosphere of intellectual twilight
in which they can only dimly discern the outlines of even their most
immediate surroundings and can be sure of nothing.

My argument here is that the lack of finality of historical proof,
though incontestable, is an improper objection to attempting historical
generalizations. In the first place it presupposes nonexistent alternatives: it suggests that there is a choice between making admittedly
vulnerable generalizations and making other statements that are
somehow sounder. Yet, by the logic of all that has been said, no such

choice exists. The objection of lack of finality applies to propositions of all kinds. The choice is not between making proved statements or unproved ones but between making unproved statements or keeping silent.

In the second place, and this is the nub of the matter, the darkness is relative. To say that all statements are uncertain is not to say that they are equally uncertain. We may not be completely sure of anything, but we can come nearer to making a convincing case for some points than for others, and we can bring some arguments to a stage where our doubts and reservations are no longer very serious and we do not feel uncomfortable in provisionally accepting certain conclusions, pending the production of evidence to the contrary, in order to get on with the work. Palmer's assertion that the epigrams of La Rochefoucauld are as much or as little verifiable as any derived from social science would appear to imply that all generalizations are verifiable, or rather unverifiable, to the same degree. Such a view disregards the fact that, measured by the admittedly necessary standard of professional consensus, some statements can be asserted with more security than others. Even if it is not possible to escape bias altogether, it may still be possible to escape it to some degree. As Ernest Nagel writes: "The very fact that biased thinking may be detected and its sources investigated shows that the case for objective explanations in history is not necessarily hopeless."[31] Though a man's own idiosyncrasies may distort his views, he must still satisfy his professional colleagues. Their personal quirks may go some distance to counteract his, and a pooling of opinions may result in rubbing away the misconceptions of individuals. This seems most likely to occur in a situation where controversy exists and where, when a man takes a position, there will be opponents on the alert to catch the loopholes in his argument. Correction of this kind seems less probable when the mistaken assumptions of an individual are shared by his entire generation. Yet even here perhaps a historian can do something to put himself on his guard by seeking to clarify his thought and purpose or to formulate his interests in propositional or categorical terms.[32] Though it is misleading to assume that proof can be final or that bias can be entirely avoided, it is also misleading to assume that the problem is impregnable on all fronts and that no inroads upon the difficulties can be made.

Such inroads have been made in many cases, and Starr's view that historians "do not now have methods by which they can reach agreement on the generalizations obtainable from a given mass of facts" seems to me too sweeping. I cannot, of course, accept his distinction between provable facts and unprovable generalizations. The point appears rather to be that such matters are relative. It might be more useful to think in terms of a scale or ladder of propositions passing from very simple statements of which we feel practically certain to increasingly complex and far-reaching statements of which we are increasingly less sure. This is not the whole story, of course, for there are other things to consider, particularly the availability of the evidence. This varies among different projects and it may actually happen that, because of better evidence, we can make a more convincing case for a complex statement on one point than for a simple statement on another. It is an objective of research design to achieve this condition, to select a problem that is not only worth studying in itself but on which, also, sufficient evidence can be found to enable the researcher to make some progress. Yet perhaps there is a rough truth, with allowance for modifying circumstances, in the notion of an inverse relationship between certainty and significance, and it may be useful to regard the question of historical generalization as revolving around this relationship.

The problem, then, is where to draw the line, how to define the most advantageous middle position between these two extremes. The proposition that generalizations should be neither too broad nor too narrow may be a defensible theoretical position, but it is not of much practical help. Yet it seems almost pointless to try to lay down any general rule. The stopping place will vary for each project: it will depend on the kind of evidence that can be found, and it will also depend on the interests and concerns of the individual, what he thinks most worth doing. Nor need the degree of reliability be the same in all cases. Some questions are important enough to be worth discussing even if our ground is not secure. There is clearly a place for intelligent speculation based on very little evidence. Perhaps it is legitimate to make generalizations at any level if they can be shown to serve a useful purpose and if no misrepresentation is made regarding the degree to which they can be substantiated.

I cannot offer a general formula in answer to this question nor can I prescribe for the profession as a whole, but I should like to express a personal opinion. This is that we may have more to gain not by extending our generalizations but by restricting them, by pursuing limited generalizations on which we have some prospect of reaching tenable ground. It seems proper to emphasize this since there has been a certain amount of talk on the other side. It is sometimes said that it is the historian's job to explain the world, for he is in a better position to do so than anyone else and that if he will not draw conclusions from his evidence others less qualified will step in and do it for him. Geoffrey Barraclough writes: "The failure of the historian to provide an interpretation of history, to say what it is all about, is another example of the notorious 'trahison des clercs', of the refusal of the specialist to live up to his work," and cites Miss Wedgwood to support his opinion.[33] Similarly, it is often urged as a criticism of the social sciences that they have increasingly abandoned the attempt to formulate large general laws, a theory of society, and now tend more to direct themselves to the detailed and often highly technical study of limited situations.

Yet I cannot see the advantage of attempting to pronounce on matters which we do not yet understand and on which our thinking and research have not progressed far enough to make a general formulation possible. I do not suggest that we should ignore the larger questions relating to the structure of society and politics that have always fascinated men. The hope of shedding some light on these points is an incentive with which we could ill afford to dispense. On the other hand, these questions are so complex that it may be better strategy to divide the enemy, to break the problems down to a point where they become more manageable. In this sense, the restriction of objectives, in history and the other social sciences, may be a sign not of degeneration but of maturity. The increased attention to smaller, more sharply defined problems which are nearer to the bottom than to the top of the scale of complexity may reflect a clearer awareness of the possibilities of these subjects and of the level at which generalizations can be most advantageously attempted.

Robert K. Merton puts the point felicitously when he speaks of focusing attention on *"theories of the middle range:* theories intermediate to the minor working hypotheses evolved in abundance during the day-by-day routines of research, and the all-inclusive speculations comprising a master conceptual scheme."[34] Contemporary sociologists who have shortened their sights and addressed themselves to the investigation of concrete problems and particular populations, who try to study simple things with high-powered instruments rather than complicated things with crude instruments, may well have strengthened their position. Though they have not offered simple solutions for complex problems, they have illuminated more limited questions in regard to which, hitherto, singularly erroneous conceptions prevailed.

Historians also may find themselves on better ground if, instead of dealing with large general problems which cannot be exactly formulated and the answers to which must be largely speculative, they consider questions on which they can hope to reach a more secure footing. The larger questions may orient our research, and it is proper that they should. They cannot, however, be solved all in a moment. We shall be digging around their roots for some time to come, and during that time our answers must continue to be incomplete and provisional. The most helpful approach to them lies in careful study, doing what we can and making sure of our ground. Little will be gained by attempting to force an answer to questions which, however important they may be, cannot be answered in the present state of our knowledge. As Paul F. Lazarsfeld has pointedly though hyperbolically remarked: "Kings who have wanted the philosopher's stone or immediate cures for currently incurable diseases have usually advanced charlatanism, not knowledge."[35]

3 THE PROBLEM OF THEORY

Here I wish to deal with the proposition that generalizations should be suggestive rather than demonstrable and that they should appeal to the imagination rather than to the external facts. Such a position does not, as I mean it, imply that the historian should fail to examine the evidence, disregard it, or openly flout it. The case is rather that, in view of the difficulties of adequate proof and the impossibility of final proof, the key to understanding the past is not the pedestrian pursuit of documentation but imagination and vision. Somewhat along this line Palmer has argued that the main purpose of a generalization should be to present an insight that helps in the understanding of a particular situation and to communicate this insight to others, "to persuade others that the view . . . is somehow more satisfactory, enlightening, or useful."

He suggests further, in a passage to which I have already briefly referred, that the penetrating observations of a brilliant man, even if subjective or impressionistic, may be more helpful than labored demonstrations which, within an inevitably limited framework, make some attempt at proof, and he argues that the maxims of La Rochefoucauld constitute generalizations "as valid, useful, and illuminating as any we are likely to get in social science, and about as much or as little capable of empirical verification by scientific method."[36]

No reply to this view will be adequate which fails to take account of the important role of unproved statements in any serious historical inquiry. It might indeed be argued that, just as the line between generalizations and facts cannot be established, so the line between proved and unproved statements, what we sometimes call generalizations and hypotheses, is also difficult to discern. If proof is merely a matter of degree, the distinction between proved and unproved statements cannot be an absolute one. Possibly all our statements, even the simplest ones, are in this sense merely working hypotheses. Some of the most useful, indeed, may not be proved or provable but merely theories of how things might work which help to explain the known evidence and do not conflict with it. It is relevant that Darwin looked at his own theory of natural selection in this light. He wrote to Herbert Spencer on February 23, 1860: "Of my numerous (private) critics, you are almost the only one who has put the philosophy of the argument, as it seems to me, in a fair way—namely, as an hypothesis (with some innate probability, as it seems to me) which explains several groups of facts."[37] It might be argued, along the same line, that the words *empirical* and *doctrinaire* are customarily used rather loosely and that probably no purely empirical research in history has even been done and no purely doctrinaire history has ever been written, though certainly impressive efforts have been made in both directions. The two terms constitute a kind of theoretical model, a pair of "ideal types," never realized in practice but convenient for purposes of analysis.

But the case may be put even more strongly. It is quite possible to produce generalizations that are wholly unverifiable and that may nevertheless prove to have considerable value. A good example can be found in the formulations of classical economics. From the foundation of modern political economy, says M. M. Postan, the tendency to abstract theorizing became increasingly predominant, so that economics formerly "tried to solve the largest possible problems from the least possible knowledge" and the ingenuity of theoretical economics was "only rivalled by the unreality of some of its conclusions." Yet modern efforts to inject larger doses of empiricism into the subject have, in the opinion of several distinguished economic historians, not helped to the degree that was expected in establishing a new formulation. The majority of these empirical studies, Postan finds, do not verify the conclusions of economic theory because most of these conclusions were so derived as to be incapable of verification or so constructed as not to require it; yet, even though unverifiable, they are illuminating and important. Commenting on the historical school of economists in Germany, Edwin F. Gay wrote that we can see now that their full hopes of inaugurating a new and more realistic stage in the development of economic science have not been realized and are not realizable. Sir John Clapham related in his inaugural lecture in 1929 that when he read Gustav Schmoller's *Principles*, a work that sought to illustrate the doctrine that "historical delineation can become economic theory," he noted on the flyleaf of his copy of the book the words, "He solves nothing." Clapham added that, "as economists, I believe that the German historical school have gone bankrupt."[38] The point I wish to make here is that there will always be things which seem important to say but which cannot be proved by the limited means of verification available to us and yet are not irresponsible or misleading but may on the contrary be significant and illuminating. We will not come to grips with the problem of generalization unless we realize that some of the most important statements we want to make must of necessity be extremely speculative.

Furthermore, it is a commonplace, not only in statistics but also in other areas of research, that an overemphasis in the direction of simple-minded empiricism is not an adequate approach and that any investigation that is worth anything must be brought under some theoretical control at an early point. As Lazarsfeld puts it: "Statistical results can be obtained only as answers to preceding speculations,"[39] and as Whitehead puts it in more general terms: "No systematic thought has made progress apart from some adequately general working hypothesis, adapted to its special topic."[40] Theory plays an essential role in intellectual advance; collection of facts by itself is inadequate and may, if theory is neglected, actually retard or impede understanding. It is unfortunately the case that a number of empirical studies have not produced results proportionate to the labor expended on them, since they were not addressed to significant problems and the objectives for which they were undertaken were insufficiently considered in theoretical terms. Indeed, the assiduous pursuit of an ostensibly strict empiricism may act as a soporific and prevent our giving critical consideration to more general problems of interpretation. It can even become a kind of escapism, a lazy man's way out, a means of avoiding the most important tasks. The mechanical parts of research are easier than the thinking parts, and the accumulation of data is easier than writing it up. An obsession with the mechanical part of the job can become an excuse for not attempting the necessary thought that should underlie it. As A. C. Bradley has said: "Research though laborious is easy; imagination though delightful is difficult."

The answer to the line of argument summarized at the outset of this section is not a flat-footed reassertion of the virtues of empiricism. It is rather, I think, the insistence on a distinction, which is not always remembered, between two kinds of intellectual activity, both needful for generalization and yet wholly different from each other: the means by which we arrive at or formulate a proposition and the means by which, once having obtained it, we attempt to assess its merits. A confusion between these two processes may lie behind a good deal of the disagreement. Those who make a great point of external checks and empirical methods may be thinking of the second stage, verification. Those who attack the uninspired collection of data, who resent quantitative techniques, who insist that historical thought must be speculative and intuitive, may be thinking of the first stage, getting ideas rather than testing or confirming them.

For the first step, deriving a generalization, no rules and no standardized procedures can be laid down. To assert that the most significant general statements are simple inductions from the evidence quite misrepresents the character of historical thinking. A generalization is not simply something logically derived from the evidence, the result of hard work effectively directed. It is also a comment on the evidence, a happy idea, an "inspiration," a new way of looking at things which helps us to understand the materials we have collected, an arrangement of the evidence in a new way so as to suggest something unexpected and important about it, the pointing-out of similarities and relation-

ships hitherto unappreciated. The most challenging problem of research is often not to collect or recite the evidence but to display the
context in which it is significant, to show how results that are trivial
or meaningless in one frame of reference may become useful or even
decisive in another.

We know relatively little about the mechanism through which
ideas occur to us. They appear to grow in the mind as we become
acquainted with the material, or perhaps as we do other quite different
things, by a process that cannot be exactly charted. A man may reach
his most important generalizations in a semi-intuitive fashion on the
basis of his general judgment of many different things which he might
find it difficult to identify. The creative process is a tangle of contradic-
tions, and an analysis of it may be more a matter of psychology than
of logic. It seems clear, however, that, while certain technical or
routine tasks can be pushed ahead in almost any circumstances, what
is needed for a real intellectual advance, for the solution of problems,
is a more intimate kind of activity and one less subject to control. Ideas
come from a variety of sources, often quite unexpected or unpromising
ones. They may be stimulated or crystallized by reading or conversation, sometimes on matters remote from and apparently quite un-
connected with the subject of inquiry. It seems, then, unwise to close
off any possible avenue of suggestion: we should be receptive to ideas
from any source and cast our nets for them as wide as is practically
possible.

I should like to mention here that, in my own research, I have found
monographic studies in the social sciences a particularly fruitful source
of inspiration and ideas. Although an interest in cooperation with the
social sciences has been identified as one of the important shifts of
emphasis in recent American historiography,[41] this change in orientation has been bitterly resented by many in the profession. It is curious
that a main objection to the use of the social sciences for historical
purposes has been that they impose mechanical and mindless methods,
techniques that are inappropriate to the complexity of historical materials, and choke up the sources of imagination and ideas. My own
experience has been precisely the opposite. I have found in this literature little that I could borrow in the way of technical devices, with
the one exception of the technique of scalogram analysis. What I have
principally gained from these materials, on the contrary, have been new

ideas and new perspectives which have enabled me to appraise my own problems differently and which have suggested questions that it might be profitable or illuminating to investigate. It seems to me unfortunate that professional limitations of outlook have prevented many historians from exploiting more fully the leads they could obtain from this impressive accumulation of ideas and findings in a related field. It appears pedantic to insist that historians must play the game according to a set of rules, that they cannot use certain procedures or approaches because they have been preempted by other disciplines, and that to attempt such borrowings is to distort by newfangled methods the clear, pure stream of historical narrative. To limit our search for ideas and methods to sources of acknowledged professional or departmental orthodoxy places an unnecessary restriction upon our efforts and serves to defeat our ultimate objectives.

As a source of ideas there is also, I like to think, a real place for the speculative essay, even if its conclusions are undemonstrable or unacceptable. Such essays, even when we disagree with them, can provide insights, suggestions, or pointers to further research. I have heard it said that we all condemn the philosophers of history—and then crib from them. This is not true, I believe, at least on any large scale, but the overemphasis illustrates the point I am trying to make. Even Pieter Geyl, Toynbee's most notable critic, has something like this to say in his essay reviewing Toynbee's last four volumes: "If one could only accept the work as a collection of stories, and glimpses of life, and dissertations on aspects and problems, from the history of the world, what a mine of curious and out-of-the-way information . . . , what flashes of insight, what instructive juxtapositions even—what learning, what brilliance!"[42] Books whose conclusions are controversial or vulnerable may, despite this, be provocative and illuminating and make, in their own way, a contribution to the progress of historical thinking that is not to be disregarded.

The second step—testing, verifying, and appraising our ideas and inspirations once we have obtained them—is obviously quite a different kind of procedure. The means by which we derive generalizations are irregular and unpredictable. The means by which we verify them are, if not altogether controlled by formal rules, at least subject to sets of assumptions and techniques that are fairly widely accepted. It has been well put that "the methods and functions of discovery and proof in research are as different as are those of a detective and of a judge in a court of law."[43] It is the essence of my argument here that in making historical generalizations the second step is as necessary as the first; that bright ideas are not enough by themselves; that generalizations even if reached intuitively should also meet the test of external verification to the satisfaction of others; and that we must reject the position that, in Sidney Hook's trenchant words, "the adequacy of the historical understanding is determined not by external criteria ... but by a self-certifying insight."[44]

It is a common experience in research that insights, though indispensable, are not always reliable. An insight may be merely euphoric and commend itself, though this may not be at first perceived, because it fits our prejudices or our present beliefs. "What is called an 'understanding' of history or of historical events is often merely the feeling of satisfaction which comes over us when a new impression or treatment of history falls easily into one or another of the categories already accepted and established in our minds."[45] Insights generally prove of unequal value; a proportion of them have to be rejected on further consideration, and many investigators have testified how large this proportion is and how many of the ideas and hypotheses that occurred to them had eventually to be discarded. The advancement of knowledge depends not only on getting ideas but also on trying them out and sifting the good ones from the bad ones.

Though theory can be a help it can also constitute a hazard. The formulation of one's ideas at too early a stage can result in a rigidity of thought from which it is difficult to escape. It is only too easy to become the prisoner of one's own preconceptions, or even of the preconceptions of the system one is attacking. The mind has a tendency to fill in, when a step in the argument is missing, with speculations or pseudo-explanations which may blind the researcher to the significance of his findings and actually impede discovery. Something like this has unquestionably happened in my own field of British political history in the nineteenth century. The developments of this period have been too often dismissed in catch phrases, and it is only recently, by hard digging and hard thinking, that some scholars have been able to advance beyond this level. Though I believe there is a place for the speculative essay, I would add to this that speculation, at least in my experience, does not prove very helpful unless it is based on considerable familiarity with the evidence and some careful thinking about it. I do not at all agree with Stuart Hughes's view that the system-builders, since they "are alone in a position to give free play to their speculative propensities, are the writers who actually operate on the 'frontiers' of historical thinking."[46] A man who tries to cover all fields is not likely to know enough about any one field to take him very far into the inwardness of events. The contributions of such writers to the problems I am interested in seem to me jejune and insipid, a secondhand rendering of the most common, if not the latest, clichés. The general studies from which I have profited have been rather different in character. For example, the explorations of Max Weber, Robert Michels, Maurice Duverger, Hannah Arendt, or David Riesman are all in part speculative and to some extent vulnerable, but they are based on significant accumulations of detailed knowledge and are directed to problems sufficiently restricted in scope so that some progress can be made in dealing with them.

The need for testing one's insights seems obvious, but it is not always remembered. My own impression is that, on the whole historians have paid too little rather than too much attention to the problem of verification of statements of any complexity. Though demanding standards of exactitude unquestionably obtain in the profession, these seem to have been addressed principally to statements of a fairly low conceptual level. As Stuart Hughes says, paraphrasing Marc Bloch: "The historian's scrupulous care in ascertaining whether an event had in fact taken place contrasted painfully with the amateurishness the same historian manifested when he came to explaining it."[47] On the other hand, the argument against pedestrianism has served as a pretext for historical methods which it seems difficult to justify by any considered standard. There still prevails a tradition of "literary history" in the bad sense, in which large, general statements jazzed up with a little swingeing rhetoric take the place of careful analysis, a procedure that seems irresponsible in the present state of our ignorance. H. A. L. Fisher, in his tribute to the Whig historians, writes that a good history is more likely to emerge "from a few first-class authorities cleverly interpreted by a fresh mind than from a vast and exhaustive miscellany of unequal value."[48] The implications suggested by this statement—that an exhaustive investigation is incompatible with

a balanced presentation and that a historian is likely to have more insight if he has not delved too deeply into his sources—give some food
for thought. Perhaps not all "literary historians" would so frankly
avow the basis of their work, but there seems to be more acceptance in
practice of Fisher's dictum than there probably would be in theory.

Historians are sometimes criticized for not venturing far enough in
the direction of generalization. A juster criticism of many historical
writers might be that they have gone too far, further at least than their
evidence warrants. Many historical works, textbooks, especially,
contain fairly wild, impressionistic general statements for which the
evidence is not, and is not likely to be, forthcoming. Nor are such
statements restricted to textbooks; writers of monographs sometimes
commit the same offense in sections where they try to orient the immediate subject of inquiry in a large context. My own interest in problems
of verification springs in part from exasperation with such goings-on.
I could not bring myself to accept many of the statements I found in
the history books. It was not merely that these statements were occasionally inconsistent; I also wondered how the authors knew or how
they could know.

For these reasons I cannot agree that the most significant statements we can make are insights and nothing more, or that the epigrams
of La Rochefoucauld, though I read them with pleasure, are as good as
we can do by way of historical generalization. I think, on the contrary,
that we can do better. La Rochefoucauld's maxims are perhaps more
fun to read than many historical monographs, partly because the
author had intelligence and wit, qualities that are unfortunately not
universally distributed in the academic profession, but partly also
because he was under no particular obligation to worry about the
validity of his generalizations and could cheerfully disembarrass himself, perhaps with a qualifying adverb, of the reservations that inevitably clutter the writings of social scientists and historians. He was free
to make impressionistic observations and, if he wished, to point them
up for effect, to call attention to a particular feature of a situation by
humorously exaggerating it. Perhaps, however, the humdrum results
of painstaking scholars who have surveyed all the available evidence
and bring us a report on it may be, though less prepossessing or less
glamorous, actually more useful for gaining an understanding of the
historical process. It should be added that it is by no means inevitable

either that the professional scholar is always pedestrian or that the amateur is always inspired.

4. THE PROBLEM OF PROCEDURE

The argument is sometimes made that, since historical understanding is a matter of insight, judgment, wisdom, and maturity, formal techniques are not particularly helpful and it is illusory to suppose that an orderly recital of the evidence, whether the order is statistical or of some different kind, will take us much further toward understanding the historical past. By this view, to suppose that the methods of historical scholarship can be gradually improved and perfected, like the internal combustion engine, is to ignore the essentially imaginative and intuitive character of historical thought. This position may be regarded as a special case of the plea for an intuitive approach to history which was discussed in the third section, and much of what I have to say in reply has been presented there. I wish to add, however, a few special points relating to questions of technique.

I take as my example statistical procedures, since these are what I know about. This is admittedly a limited subject because elaborate statistics are not appropriate for many, perhaps the great majority, of historical problems, and it is a mistake to force the use of the method when the data will not sustain it. Also, the method, even in cases where it can be applied, is laborious: the problems of gathering, classifying, manipulating, and interpreting the materials for statistical work are more formidable than will probably be appreciated by anyone who has not attempted this kind of research. Despite these difficulties statistics can perhaps offer certain advantages in subjects where they can properly be used, and I do not think that their value for historical purposes has been sufficiently explored or that enough attention has been given to the possibility of making verifiable generalizations through the formal arrangement of evidence. This subject has been more fully discussed in the preceding chapter. I wish to take advantage of certain points made there, and to add some further comments, in order to bring out more fully the way in which the use of quantitative methods can help with the problem of generalization.

Quantitative procedures seem particularly to raise the hackles of a large section of the history profession, and the objections to new and unfamiliar methods have been directed with a special virulence against statistics. Protests have come from outside the history profession as well—for example, from C. Wright Mills in *The Sociological Imagination* —and the value of some of the monumental quantitative studies that have been conducted in the United States over the last two decades is still energetically disputed in certain quarters. There have in general been two lines of attack upon statistical enterprises: that their findings are trivial or unimportant, and that their conclusions are unproved or incorrect. It is argued that such studies have been too limited in outlook, that they have dealt with insignificant problems merely because they could be investigated, and that the broader questions which really matter are apparently not amenable to this kind of treatment. It is also argued that the precision of techniques cannot compensate for the inexactitude of the raw data, that the crudeness of our observations and the vagueness of our fundamental categories will not be cured by manipulation of the paraphernalia of statistical methods, and that any significant conelusions reached by such means must depend on a chain of shaky reasoning that is too long and too vulnerable for the conclusions to be accepted with any degree of 'assurance.[49]

Richard Hofstadter has formulated what he calls the "paradox of quantification" arising from the apparent inconclusiveness of quantitative studies:

The essence of this paradox is that the recent use of quantitative methods to test historical generalization has resulted in the wholesale destruction of categories that previously held sway in the historian's vocabulary without supplanting them with new generalizations of comparable significance. . . . It is, of course, quite conceivable that the uprooted generalizations will be replaced by interpretations having a more social-psychological cast. But in such case it is unlikely that the historian can, with the type of evidence available to him, put these interpretations on any better footing than that of intelligent and partially verified guesses. Should this be true, we might find ourselves in possession of more sophisticated and seemingly more satisfactory explanations which would have to stand largely upon a speculative foundation.[50]

It must be confessed that quantitative research can be discouraging. One finds trends that contribute, so far as they go, to confirm or refute certain hypotheses, but the very investigations that reveal the trends also reveal important exceptions to them that must be explained as well. It is also well understood that statistics prove nothing and that the results of a statistical investigation may be undependable for reasons unrelated to the quality of the mathematics in it. Every statistical presentation includes two nonstatistical steps: (1) the assumptions, and the collection of data based on these assumptions, at the beginning; and (2) the inferences at the end. Both steps contain pitfalls. The detailed data available for any large historical project will almost certainly be incomplete and partly inaccurate, and this fact imposes an inevitable limitation on the conclusions ultimately drawn from them. Furthermore, the inferences at the end are not "proved" by the statistics; they are in fact not statistical *statements* at all; they are *logically inferred*, and their reliability is determined not by arithmetic but by whether we can make a persuasive case for them. This is not to say that they are nonsense, but they are matters of logic and judgment, not of figures, and for this reason no statistical treatment of a problem can ever be entirely objective. These points are, of course, no news. They are commonplaces, to be found in all the standard manuals of statistics. Statisticians are as alert to them as nonstatisticians, more so, indeed, since the formal structure of their argument necessitates a more explicit formulation. Such objections are generally regarded, and correctly, as serving to mark the boundaries of what statistics can do, rather than to discredit the method. After all these points have been allowed for, much is still feasible.

In the first place, an orderly arrangement of the evidence is a major step toward coming to terms with it, as anyone knows who has had to do desk work of any kind, scholarly or administrative. A systematic arrangement of this kind can sometimes carry further than appeared possible at the outset of the investigation for, as we work into a problem, we sometimes find that certain information proves usable in ways not expected when we first encountered it. A formal arrangement also helps to achieve a greater degree of objectivity. Setting up categories for classifying the evidence necessitates some careful thought about their meaning and relevance and in this way imposes on the investigator the burden of clarifying his ideas and defining his assumptions more explicitly. Most important, a formal quantitative arrangement of the evidence forces upon the investigator's attention the discrepancies between theories and observation, the points at which they do not correspond, in a particularly obtrusive fashion. As Robert K. Merton says, the quantitative anomaly, unlike many qualitative ones, cannot be easily evaded.[51] The very nakedness of the results, the intolerable character of a discrepancy of this kind, acts as a stimulus to reformulation and may also give a good indication of the direction in which it can best be attempted.

Hofstadter's insistence that statistics are destructive rather than constructive, that they do not replace the generalizations they overturn with new formulations of comparable significance, suggests the implication, though this may not have been intended, that generalizations are useful only when they are absolute or invariant. If this were true, statistics, since they generally show exceptions to every rule, could scarcely provide adequate support for generalizations. The usual experience of historians, however, seems to be that absolute or invariant hypotheses are almost never confirmed and that few general statements of any significance are completely true. What is most useful is not to establish the truth or the falsity of a particular general statement but to determine the extent to which it holds, the exact degree of the trend. Historians deal with a universe not of absolutes but of probabilities, and for a world conceived in these terms statistics are the appropriate tool.

It is essential to make a distinction between a sweeping general statement to which no limits are set and a generalization that is based on a measurable comparison. The comment by Proust, quoted earlier (p. 77), regarding the unwillingness of men to alter their beliefs in the light of the facts may serve as an illustration. Proust's statement at once commends itself, for it seems amply confirmed by other observations we have made; most readers would be able to cite illustrations of it from their own experience. Yet it is obvious on a moment's thought that the proposition does not invariably hold and that the degree of illusion is not the same in all cases. One begins to wonder, on further thought, how frequently this kind of thing happens, to what sorts of people, in what sorts of circumstances, and how far the degree of self-deception varies in different cases. These are questions of a different kind, and they require an answer stated in comparative and, if possible, measurable terms. I should argue that general or sweeping statements that include no qualification are actually less informative than statements based on a comparison and that once we stop asking whether a given statement is true and inquire instead how far it is true the argument reaches a new level not only of reliability but also of significance.

A final point should be made in regard to the proposition that statistics are destructive rather than constructive, that they tear down generalizations instead of building them up. I cannot accept the view that to test a hypothesis and find it does not work simply leads to a dead end. Negative results, the exclusion of *unacceptable* hypotheses, are always useful; and in some contexts they can be as significant as positive results. Nor have the results of statistical inquiries always been purely negative.[52] For example, the statistical studies of voting behavior over the last generation have enormously deepened and improved our understanding of the nature of political choice and the mechanism of a political system. Though much still remains to be elucidated, the discussion of these questions now takes place on a level of knowledge and understanding, based on the patient accumulation of evidence, that would have been impossible thirty years ago. Beyond this, a refinement of the evidence and of the techniques of measuring evidence has often proved highly rewarding in terms of new discoveries.

Of course, no presentation is final, all measurements and descriptions are accurate to only a limited degree, all investigations are incomplete, and in any formulation of the results of research there will always be what P. W. Bridgman has happily termed a "penumbra of uncertainty." As Bridgman goes on to say, however, it is exactly within this penumbra of uncertainty that the important new advances are often made.[53] Something like this may be true for the study of history and of political behavior. Certainly I have had some pleasant confirmations of this in my own experience, to an extent altogether beyond what I had originally anticipated. The statistical method, though it is not in general regarded as an empirical one, can in this sense have a heuristic value. In an area where one has already given a good deal of thought to the evidence and to the assumptions involved in handling it, material gathered to test a particular thesis may not merely refute the thesis but also point the way to a new and more appropriate formulation. Exact measurements may sometimes provide new insights and new perspectives that one could gain in no other way. It may be granted that our present knowledge is relative and imperfect and our present measurements are inexact, but it does not follow from this that nothing will be gained by more exhaustive study and more accurate measurements. The arbitrary rejection of techniques for refining the evidence and making our grasp of it more precise not only fails to cure the disease but aggravates it; it works directly against our best hope for a further understanding of our problems.

NOTES

1. Hans Reichenbach, *The Rise of Scientific Philosophy* (1951; new ed.; Berkeley and Los Angeles: University of California Press, 1958), p. 6.

2. *Laws and Explanation in History* (New York: Oxford University Press, 1957).

3. "The Historian's Use of Generalization," in Leonard D. White (ed.), *The State of the Social Sciences* ... (Chicago: University of Chicago Press, 1956), p. 437.

4. "The Study of National Character...," *Harvard Library Bulletin,* **XIII** (1959), p. 7.

5. *Historical Inevitability* (New York: Oxford University Press, 1954), p. 70.

6. "Evidence and Inference in History," in Daniel Lerner (ed.), *Evidence and Inference: The Hayden Colloquium on Scientific Concept and Method* (Glencoe, Ill.: Free Press, 1959), p. 19.

7. "Problems of Terminology in Historical Writing—Illustrations," *Theory and Practice in Historical Study* (SSRC Bulletin 54), p. 124.

8. *Doubt and Certainty in Science: A Biologist's Reflections on the Brain* (New York: Oxford University Press, 1951), pp. 61—66.

9. Hook, *Op. cit.,* p. 127. Hook uses this quotation to illustrate his definition of the term *generalization.*

10. Wallace Notestein, *The Winning of the Initiative by the House of Commons: The Raleigh Lecture on History* (London: Oxford University Press, 1924), p. 17.

11. Lewis B. Namier, *Monarchy and the Party System: The Romanes Lecture* (Oxford: Clarendon, 1952), p. 4.

12. Walter Bagehot, *The English Constitution* (1867; new ed.; London: Oxford University Press, 1928), pp. 260—61.

13. Robert Michels, *Political Parties: A Sociological Study of the Oligarchical Tendencies of Modern Democracy* (English trans.; New York: Hearst's International Library, 1915), p. 12.

14. Arthur M. Schlesinger, Jr., *The Vital Center* (Boston: Houghton Mifflin, 1949), p. 51.

15. Crane Brinton, *Ideas and Men: The Story of Western Thought* (New York: Prentice-Hall, 1950), p. 442.

16. Letters to the Committee, Jan. 29, 1959, and June 16, 1958 in Louis Gottschalk, ed., *Generalization in the Writing of History: A Report of the Committee on Historical Analysis of the Social Science Research Council* (Chicago, 1963), pp. 76, 75.

17. "Reflections upon the Problem of Generalization," in Gottschalk, *Generalization in the Writing of History*, pp. 3, 15—18.

18. Quoted in Ernst Cassirer, *The Myth of the State* (New Haven: Yale University Press, 1946; new ed.; Garden City, N.Y.: Doubleday, 1955), p. 282.

19. See the discussion by James L. Cate, "Humanism and the Social Sciences: But What about John de Neushom?" in White, pp. 429—30.

20. *Debates with Historians* (1955; rev. ed.; New York: Meridian, 1958), chaps. v—viii and "Toynbee's Answer," *Mededelingen der Koninklijke Nederlandse Akademie van Wetenschappen, afd. Letterkunde*, **XXIV** (1961), pp. 181—204.

21. *Op. cit.*, p. 69.

22. *Debates with Historians*, p. 283. See, for similar cases, the contrast between the learned and the public reaction to Spengler described by H. Stuart Hughes, *Oswald Spengler: A Critical Estimate* (New York: Scribner's, 1952), pp. 1—2 and the contrast between the scientific and the popular reception of Robert Chambers' *Vestiges of Creation* discussed by Milton Millhauser, *Just before Darwin: Robert Chambers and Vestiges* (Middletown, Conn.: Wesleyan University Press, 1959), pp. 116—40.

23. "Arnold J. Toynbee's Philosophy of History," *Journal of Modern History*, **XII** (1940), p. 374. It should be added, however, that Sorokin is also highly critical of certain features of Toynbee's work.

24. "Historical Knowledge: A Review Article on the Philosophy of History," *Journal of Modern History*, **XXXI** (1959), p. 247.

25. "The 'New History' and 'Past Everything,'" *American Scholar*, **VIII** (1939), p. 153.

26. Morris R. Cohen, "Reason in Social Science," in Herbert Feigl and May Brodbeck (eds.), *Readings in the Philosophy of Science* (New York: Appleton-Century-Crofts, 1953), pp. 663—69; Edgar Zilsel, "Physics and the Problem of Historico-Sociological Laws," *ibid.*, pp. 715—16 and 720.

27. "Some Problems Raised by Historical Relativism," *Journal of Modern History*, **XXI** (1949), p. 17.

28. Schlesinger, *Op. cit.*, p. 49.

29. *The Philosophy of History in Our Time* ... (Garden City, N.Y.: Doubleday, 1959), p. 161.

30. Pieter Geyl, *Use and Abuse of History* (New Haven: Yale University Press, 1955), pp. 60—61.

31. "The Logic of Historical Analysis," in Meyerhoff, p. 213. Willson H. Coates has acutely suggested: "Once we have stamped finality as the great heresy for scholars, we can see the concept of the relativity of knowledge as a movement in the direction of greater objectivity." The relativists, he says, by successfully challenging historical "objectivity" put history " in a philosophic perspective which is a nearer approach to the objectivity which they deny is possible." ("Relativism and the Use of Hypothesis in History," *Journal of Modern History*, **XXI** [1949], p. 24).

32. See "Proposition VIII" in SSRC Bulletin 54, pp. 135—36, and also Thomas C. Cochran, "A Survey of Concepts and Viewpoints in the Social Sciences," *The Social Sciences in Historical Study* (SSRC Bulletin 64), p. 85.

33. *History in a Changing World* (Oxford: Blackwell, 1955), p. 222. H. Stuart Hughes advances a similar argument in "The Historian and the Social Scientist," *American Historical Review*, **LXVI** (1960), p. 45.

34. *Social Theory and Social Structure* (1949; rev. and enlarged ed.; Glencoe, Ill.: Free Press, 1957), pp. 5—6.

35. Rose K. Goldsen *et al., What College Students Think* (Princeton: Van Nostrand, 1960), p. xi.

36. Letter to the Committee, June 16, 1958, Gottschalk, *Generalization in the Writing of History*, p. 75.

37. Quoted in David Duncan, *Life and Letters of Herbert Spencer* (2 vols.; New York: Appleton, 1908), **I**, p. 128.

38. M. M. Postan, *The Historical Method in Social Science: An Inaugural Lecture* (Cambridge: At the University Press, 1939), sections I and II; Edwin F. Gay, "The Tasks of Economic History," *Journal of Economic History*, **I**, Supplement (December, 1941), pp. 9—16; J. H. Clapham, *The Study of Economic History: An Inaugural Lecture* (Cambridge: At the University Press, 1929), pp. 30—31.

39. Paul F. Lazarsfeld *et al., The People's Choice* ... (New York: Columbia University Press, 1944), p. 42.

40. This quotation from Alfred North Whitehead is used by Lee Benson as an epigraph to his book, *Turner and Beard: American Historical Writing Reconsidered* (Glencoe, Ill.: Free Press, 1960).

41. SSRC Bulletin 64, pp. 13—14 and 21.

42. *Debates with Historians,* pp. 181—82.

43. W. I. B. Beveridge, *The Art of Scientific Investigation* (1950; rev. ed.; New York: Norton, 1957), p. 123.

44. Hook, *Op. cit.,* p. 128.

45. "Proposition XIII" in SSRC Bulletin 54, p. 137.

46. "The Historian and the Social Scientist," p. 27.

47. *Ibid.,* p. 21.

48. *The Whig Historians: The Raleigh Lecture on History* (London: Oxford University Press, 1928), p. 28.

49. C. Wright Mills, *The Sociological Imagination* (New York: Oxford University Press, 1959), Chap. 3; Nathan Glazer, "'The American Soldier' as Science: Can Sociology Fulfill Its Ambitions?" *Commentary,* **VIII** (1949), pp. 487—96; Cohen, pp. 663—65.

50. "History and the Social Sciences," in Fritz Stern (ed.), *Varieties of History: From Voltaire to the Present* (New York: Meridian, 1956), p. 415, n. 14. Hofstadter's comment has also been discussed in Chapter 2, pp. 56—57.

51. "The History of Quantification in the Sciences: Report on a Conference," *Items,* **XIV** (1960), p. 3.

52. Hofstadter, when he speaks of the failure of statistics to supplant old categories with new generalizations of comparable significance, cites as one of his sources an article which I published some years ago in which I laid a good deal of emphasis on the point that the complexity of the evidence worked against simple formulations. The results of my research since then have proved more encouraging, and I have shifted my position to one of somewhat greater, though still guarded, optimism. See, for example, two recent articles of mine, the first dealing with problems of stratification and the second dealing with problems of political behavior: "The Business Interests of the Gentry in the Parliament of 1841—47," published as an appendix in G. Kitson Clark, *The Making of Victorian England* (London: Methuen, 1962), pp. 290—305; and "Voting Patterns in the British House of Commons in the 1840s," *Comparative Studies in Society and History,* **V,** no. 2 (January, 1963), pp. 134—163.

53. *The Logic of Modern Physics* (1927; new ed.; New York: Macmillan, 1960), pp. 33—34.

CHAPTER 4

A DATA ARCHIVE FOR MODERN
BRITISH POLITICAL HISTORY[1]

Over the last several decades there has been a rapidly developing interest in the study of British political history by quantitative means. Scholars have come increasingly to realize that the collection of large amounts of data, and their presentation in tabular form, may be used to advance the discussion of certain types of problems that could not properly be dealt with in other ways. Yet, though significant work has already been done, scholars in this area have been under a handicap. Assembling information for such investigations is immensely laborious, and the lack of readily available collections of quantitative data in a suitable form has placed limitations on research and has made it difficult to follow up certain promising lines of investigation. In this respect students of British history are at a disadvantage as compared to students of American history. Vigorous efforts have been made in the United States to meet these needs with various collections of information, the most notable of which is the immense volume of materials now being assembled by the Inter-University Consortium for Political Research at Ann Arbor, Michigan. I wish to raise the question whether it would be possible to attempt a similar enterprise for Great Britain: to collect, for British political history in the nineteenth and twentieth centuries, data in machine-readable form comparable, so far as circumstances permit, to the data for American political history in the same period which are now being gathered by the Consortium.

The Consortium, in addition to providing special information for individual projects, has undertaken three large general programs, the collection of electoral, roll-call, and demographic data.

1. It is gathering and processing county-level returns for elections to the four offices of president, governor, and United States senator and representative. These county returns will be summed to constituency totals. Plans are also being considered for assembling information on selected state referenda—it is estimated that there have been between 15,000 and 20,000 of these[2]—and on primary elections in southern states.

2. It is also recording and processing the votes of all individuals in all roll calls in both houses of Congress from the Continental Congresses to the present.

3. It is assembling data on demographic conditions from the published United States Census Reports from 1790 to the present, and will, presumably, try to obtain such information from other sources as well. These data, which are mostly at the county level, will be summed to the congressional district level and the state level.

To follow this example for Great Britain would be an immense undertaking. Even so, it would be restricted: This is only one of a number of lines that the collection of quantitative data could take. In the first place, such an enterprise, with its focus on political history, would make only limited contributions to social and economic history, two areas of British studies where a good deal of active quantifying is already going on.[3] Nor would it embrace all the possibilities for the collection of quantitative data even in political history. Local authority elections in Britain have attracted the attention of several scholars and are clearly of great interest,[4] though their incorporation in the present scheme would constitute an almost unmanageably large addition to an already huge project. Possibly use could be made, for electoral data, of information in the surviving poll-books. Votes in parliament, particularly as party discipline has increased, are not always revealing, and might be supplemented by other types of information that would yield more direct clues to the opinions of members. Punch-cards could also be used to record information about the personal backgrounds of members of parliament and could serve, in this way, as the basis for analyses of the composition, collective biographies, of parliament in different periods. On this last point a good deal of interesting work has already been done, though not always with punch-cards.

Yet, though there are many attractive possibilities for collecting quantitative data, there is also something to be said for imposing restrictions. Efforts to collect such materials are more likely to be successful if directed toward limited objectives, and a program that is too broad or too ambitious may be self-defeating. Although the possibilities of quantitative research in social and economic history are by no means exhausted, the need for assembling materials in political history is also great. It is true that a significant start has been made and that valuable data have been collected by several English scholars including David Butler, Henry Pelling, B. R. Mitchell, Richard Rose, Hugh Berrington and a number of others. If the project suggested here should be undertaken, every effort should be made to take advantage of the knowledge and experience of these individuals and of any assistance that they are willing to give. The other side of the picture, however, is that work along this line has been impeded by the lack of a large and readily available collection of basic data and that, for this reason, those who have pioneered in the field have been operating under difficulties.

Within the field of political history, in spite of the variety of possibilities, there are arguments for attempting to follow the Consortium's precedent that appear to have some weight. The limits this sets are not in any case stringent: The program suggested here is in itself so large that there may be a real question whether it can ever be carried through. Also, whatever other types of information might be considered for inclusion, there can be little question that the three kinds of data now being assembled by the Consortium are essential for the study and understanding of any parliamentary system. It is an additional consideration that following the precedent of the Consortium might make possible some interesting comparisons. The complaint is frequently made, and it is well-justified, that historians working on similar problems in different fields or in different periods do not ask the same questions and that, as a result, their findings cannot be compared and the gain in cumulative knowledge that might have been expected does not occur. The value of comparative studies, when circumstances permit them, has been increasingly appreciated; indeed a journal devoted to such studies has been established and is now published from Ann Arbor. It should not be left out of account that following the example of the Consortium would make it possible to benefit from what those associated with that enterprise have learned during the six years in which it has been in operation. The Consortium, though its work is far from complete, has already advanced so far that it can scarcely avoid being regarded, to some extent at least, as a model by those engaged in similar enterprises. Its staff has, in fact, been increasingly drawn into an advisory function, into the work of providing technical suggestions to other organizations on the full range of problems of data handling, and has come to regard this work as part of its normal task.[5]

1 ELECTORAL DATA

In any democratic or parliamentary system, elections are presumed to constitute the principal machinery through which the nation at large is able to exert control over those who govern it. Though it is now clear that this control is more complex in nature and more ambiguous in impact than it was once believed to be, it is still in a sense true that information about elections forms the basic data of political history. Students of national politics or of legislative behavior naturally wish to know something of the local circumstances in the constituencies where the elections took place. They will be concerned about such matters as, for example, whether a contest occurred, the nature of the party competition, the extent of malapportionment, and the degree of political participation by the electorate.

Of the various categories of elections on which the Consortium is gathering data for the United States—the elections of president, governor, senator, and so forth—all but one are irrelevant for British politics. There is, in Great Britain, no presidential election, since the prime minister is chosen by the sovereign with the approval of parliament. There is nothing to correspond to the election of a governor, since there is no local office of comparable importance. There is nothing similar to the election of a senator, since the upper house is not elective. American state referenda and primary elections do not have significant parallels in Great Britain. The only elections in Great Britain that can be studied in this way are the elections to the House of Commons. Those concerned with British electoral data need to study only one set of elections, not four or more, and this would seem to constitute an initial simplification of the task.

Furthermore, information on how many votes were cast for each candidate in each local election is usually, though not always, easy to get. It can be obtained from a number of convenient sources that can be checked against each other, so far as this proves necessary.[6] Information about by-elections does not always appear in such sources; these are often, however, reported in the newspapers. B. R. Mitchell and Klaus Boehm, in their survey of electoral results since 1950, were able to obtain additional information about by-elections from the Librarian of *The Times* and from the electoral registration officers of a number of constituencies. It is also an advantage that for British elections the problem does not arise, as it does for the Consortium, of summing county-level returns to constituency totals; it is the contituency totals that are given in the first place.

There seems no reason at present to expect unusual difficulties in processing this information. It might be supposed that party labels would be troublesome, since a good many different ones have appeared in British politics over the last two centuries and, in addition, a number of candidates have claimed to be independent. A conscientious scholar might find himself burdened with an uncomfortably large number of party categories. It turns out, however, that the Consortium is now working with well over 800 individual party labels and with many unaffiliated candidates as well. (Candidates are, of course, recorded by name as well as by party.) If such a variety can be managed for American political history, presumably it can be for British political history, too. There might also be a question about the feasibility of processing, in addition to the results of general elections, the results of by-elections occurring at irregular times. On this point, as well, the experience of the Consortium is reassuring. I am informed that the Consortium has had some difficulty in recovering data for by-elections but that including this information, once it is obtained, in the data archive has created no special problems.

The difficulties of handling British electoral statistics are of a quite different kind. They do not relate to finding the information and tabulating it, which appear to be relatively easy matters. They arise, rather, from the character of the British electoral system which is, or at least has been, different from the American one in important respects. As a result of these differences, electoral information cannot be used for scholarly purposes in quite the same way, and some of the things commonly done with the American data cannot be done with the British.

Problems develop particularly when an attempt is made to appraise the general or national political situation.

There are, first, the matters of the "multiple vote" and the "plural vote." In multiple-member constituencies, until 1867, each elector had as many votes as there were members for the constituency. In 1867 multiple voting was reduced though not eliminated; voters in three-member constituencies, for example, now had only two votes instead of three. Multiple voting almost disappeared in 1885, when single-member constituencies were made nearly universal. Yet eighteen two-member constituencies and even one three-member constituency (the Scottish universities) survived until the legislation of 1948, so that the first general election in which there was *no* multiple voting whatsoever was that of 1950. This feature of the British electoral system makes it difficult, for most of the nineteenth century, to get any clear idea of the toal number of individuals that supported any party. One cannot simply add together the votes in the various constituencies, since a vote might represent one elector, half an elector, one-third, or even one-fourth. The number of votes cast will in any case be much greater than the number of electors who voted. Nor is the number of votes in a constituency with two or more members even a multiple of the number of electors who voted, because of the prevalence of the practice of "plumping", by which an elector could give one of his votes to one candidate but withhold or not cast his other vote or votes. An elector could not cast more than one vote for a single candidate but, having done this, he was at liberty to refrain from exercising his privilege to vote for anyone else, and it was of course advantageous to his candidate that he should do so. In some elections, in some constituencies, the number of plumpers is known from a contemporary source that has survived, such as a poll book, and D. C. Moore and J. R. Vincent have done interesting work with this material.[7] When this information is not available, it is difficult to determine the number of electors who supported either side. It is also difficult to determine the extent of political participation by the electorate, since it is hard to be sure just how many electors voted. It is a further complication that the system might and frequently did result in the return of candidates of opposite political persuasions from the same constituency, often without a contest;[8] this possibility makes the determination of party loyalty or political affiliation in that constituency an ambiguous matter.

It was also possible that a single individual might vote in more than one constituency. Plural voting, in the sense of the business vote and the university vote, did not altogether disappear until 1948. In certain circumstances, a man with a home in one constituency and a business establishment in another could vote in both. Also, some of those who voted in the constituencies in which they lived could vote in university constituencies as well, provided that they belonged to the group of "Electors, Doctors, and Masters of Arts whose names are on the books." Since the incidence of plural voting may not be easy to calculate, this is another factor that can distort regional or national summations.

The most serious problem, however, is that of elections which were uncontested or not fully contested. It is often not possible to say what the vote was in a given constituency in a given general election because there was no vote. In many cases only one candidate presented himself for each seat, he was returned unopposed, and no contest occurred. The problem here is not that it is difficult to recover the data but, rather, that the data do not exist; the events that could have generated them never took place. Since there is no point in setting up a large project to collect nonexistent information, the question of the exact incidence of contests in the period since 1832 is crucial. I have assembled this information and presented it in Table I. Norman Gash has pointed out that "it is surprisingly difficult to get agreed figures of contested elections" for the period 1832—1847,[9] and this is true also for the succeeding decades. The figures it proved possible to reach with the sources available to me do not invariably coincide with those presented by other students, who indeed often do not agree with each other, but the differences are in all cases small, and the general picture stands out clearly enough.[10]

From Table I it appears that, until the election of 1880, the proportion of uncontested seats was always more than one-fourth and that in the 1840's and 1850's it was often more than one-half. After the mid-nineteenth century the proportion of uncontested seats gradually decreased but, with the exceptions of the elections of 1885 and 1892, it remained considerable until after the first World War. Since then, 90 per cent or more of the seats have generally been contested, though the first election in British history in which contests took place in *every* constituency was that of 1955, a fact that attracted some attention at the time. These figures do not, however, tell the whole story; and the num-

TABLE I
Uncontested seats, 1832–1964

Year of general election	Number of uncontested seats	Total number of seats	Percentage of seats uncontested
1832	189	658	28.7
1835	271	658	41.2
1837	234	658	35.6
1841	336	658	51.1
1847	368	656	56.1
1852	257	654	39.3
1857	330	654	50.5
1859	379	654	58.0
1865	301	658	45.7
1868	210	658	31.9
1874	187	652	28.7
1880	108	652	16.6
1885	44	670	6.6
1886	224	670	33.4
1892	63	670	9.4
1895	188	670	28.1
1900	243	670	36.3
1906	113	670	16.9
1910 Jan.	75	670	11.2
1910 Dec.	162	670	24.2
1918	107	707	15.1
1922	57	615	9.3
1923	50	615	8.1
1924	32	615	5.2
1929	7	615	1.1
1931	65	615	10.6
1935	40	615	6.5
1945	3	640	0.5
1950	2	625	0.3
1951	4	625	0.6
1955	0	630	0.0
1959	0	630	0.0
1964	0	630	0.0

ber of seats effectively contested by the two major parties was, during a considerable part of the nineteenth century, even less. As H. J. Hanham has pointed out, some seats were contested only by rival candidates of the same party, while others in two-member constituencies were virtually uncontested because the weaker party put up only one candidate. Also, the development of the Home Rule movement put an end to contests in Ireland between Liberals and Conservatives, except in the smallest boroughs and in Ulster, since one party usually withdrew and left the other to fight the Home Rulers. Hanham estimates, on the basis of some figures he has presented in a table, that "about half the 650-odd seats were either absolutely uncontested or virtually uncontested in 1868 and 1874, and about two-fifths of them in 1880."[11] Until one begins to deal with elections occurring after the first World War, it is extremely difficult to make reliable estimates of the total national support for either party. Hanham has argued persuasively that nineteenth-century elections bear only superficial resemblance to twentieth-century ones, and that comparisons between the two are largely meaningless. This is not only because election registers and election results were more carelessly prepared or recorded in the last century; it is principally because general elections in the period he discusses were not general, since only about half the seats were contested by both parties. Such comparisons, he holds, can be made only for the minority of constituencies in the nineteenth century that were contested at every election by enough candidates to make it clear that the contest was a party one as well as a local one.[12]

Students of British politics have, of course, turned their attention to these problems; and statistical devices have been worked out to deal with them and to make appropriate corrections in the total figures. Yet an element of uncertainty, the exact size of which is difficult to calculate, still remains.[13] This feature of the situation, the inevitable incompleteness of British electoral data, may well raise some question as to how far an expensive program of assembling such data for the nineteenth and twentieth centuries could be justified.

The other side of the argument, however, is that, for any subject or for any period of history, one must make do with what one has. Although a realistic assessment of the difficulties should be made at the outset, the question should also be asked whether the materials at hand are still sufficiently abundant to furnish some solid basis for study. The answer to this question is clearly in the affirmative, as, indeed, Hanham's own suggestive manipulations of nineteenth-century election figures go far to show. It should not be forgotten that the lack of occurrence of a contest in a given constituency is itself a significant datum, and that even contests between candidates of the same party may be worth studying.

Consideration should also be given to including in the data archive some types of electoral information that are peculiar to British politics and that it would not be appropriate to collect for the United States. One feature of great interest is the extent of electoral influence but this, though its existence and importance are indubitable, was so various in its manifestations and so difficult to appraise exactly that it would be almost impossible to quantify. Figures on the size of the electorate and the size of the population for each constituency, on the other hand, are easy to get and could be included. From these figures some interesting ratios could readily be derived which perhaps should be calculated—a simple matter—and incorporated in the data. The ratio of the electorate to the number of seats and the ratio of the population to the number of seats, for each constituency, would make useful crude indexes of malapportionment. The ratio of the population to the electorate would give an indication of the impact of the franchise requirements in different types of constituencies and, for constituencies of the same type, would give some indication of how large a segment of the population could meet these requirements—it was in the mid-nineteenth century, far less in southern Ireland, for example, than in other parts of the United Kingdom. I have had figures on these three points prepared for the entire country, which are shown for illustrative purposes in Table II. They could easily be prepared for individual constituencies and should be, since the local variations in these respects at any one time could be extensive.

2 THE DIVISION LISTS

For the study of the attitudes and opinions of the British political elite the division lists, though they have hitherto been surprisingly little exploited for research purposes, are an extraordinarily rich source. They relate to major questions of the day, they are voluminous and give ample and repeatedly corroborated information, they are remarkably

TABLE II

Variations in Relationships Between Size of Electorate, Size of Population, and Number of Seats in House of Commons

Year	Ratio of Electorate to Number of Seats	Ratio of Population to Number of Seats	Ratio of Population to Electorate
1832	1,230	37,132	30.19
1835	1,277	38,198	29.92
1837	1,465	38,983	26.62
1841	1,594	40,592	25.47
1847	1,728	42,640	24.67
1852	1,810	41,970	23.18
1857	1,843	43,100	23.39
1859	1,936	43,717	22.59
1865	2,063	45,479	22.04
1868	3,764	46,641	12.39
1874	4,327	49,849	11.52
1880	4,617	53,103	11.50
1885	8,219	53,755	6.54
1886	8,462	54,199	6.41
1892	9,185	56,916	6.20
1895	9,451	58,539	6.19
1900	10,046	61,425	6.11
1906	10,843	64,718	5.97
1910 Jan.	11,485	67,039	5.84
1910 Dec.	11,507	67,564	5.87
1918	30,258	61,229	2.02
1922	34,354	72,150	2.10
1923	34,604	72,515	2.10
1924	35,335	73,034	2.07
1929	46,912	74,263	1.58
1931	48,717	74,919	1.54
1935	51,023	76,210	1.49
1945	51,307	76,847	1.50
1950	54,832	80,986	1.48
1951	55,433	80,360	1.45
1955	55,331	80,902	1.45
1959	56,186	82,517	1.47
1964	56,972	85,238	1.50

NOTE: The figures in Table II cannot be accepted as entirely exact, partly because it is known that there were many inaccuracies in the returns of the numbers of registered electors, and partly because general elections often do not coincide with Census years and, when this is the case, it is necessary to rely on contemporary estimates of the size of the population.

accurate and reliable, as historical sources go, and they give comparable information for a large number of individuals, the members of the House of Commons. Their possible value was suggested many years ago by President Lowell of Harvard in a monograph published in the annual report of the American Historical Association for 1901.[14] His study, though crude by present-day standards, was imaginative and forward-looking, and anticipated in an interesting way some of the trends of modern research. Yet his work was not extensively followed up; and it is only comparatively recently that scholars have begun again to address themselves to the kinds of questions that could be answered with such information. Historians now have more powerful analytical tools, largely supplied by workers in other disciplines, with which to come to terms with these great masses of material. They also have the aid of computers, if they want them and will learn how to use them. What they do not have is the information itself, which is so voluminous and so laborious to collect that a single individual, working with limited time and money, can scarcely hope to assemble even all the evidence relevant to his own subject of study.

Information on the divisions is easily available, at least from 1836 when the House of Commons commenced publication of its own division lists. Hansard also gives division lists but, for the early nineteenth century, its information is incomplete. For 1836, for example, the first year of publication of the official lists, Hansard gives 128 divisions, and of these only 110 were recorded entire; for 18 the votes on only one side were listed. The official published list, on the other hand, gives 187 divisions for 1836.[15] There is a copy of the published lists of divisions in the House of Commons, from 22 February 1836 through August 1897, in the Library of the Institute of Historical Research in London, of which I have had a microfilm made for the University of Iowa Library. I have used these lists in preparing this report but, for the period after 1897, where Hansard appears, so far as I have been able to check it, much more complete, I have used only Hansard.

It might be best to begin the tabulation of divisions in the House of Commons with 1836, the first year of the publication of the official lists. Professor Donald Ginter of Duke University is collecting information on early divisions in the House of Commons, and intends to bring his survey down at least through the general election of 1830, and possibly further. The present project should, in any case, be set up so as to mesh with his and to avoid leaving a no-man's-land in between. If the years 1830—1835 are not to be included in his project, they could be incorporated into this one. It does not make much difference, since there are only a limited number of divisions in these years on which information can be obtained, and including them would not involve a large addition to the task. Arrangements should be made so that the materials before 1830 and after it are placed in the same data collection and punched in such a way that they can be mechanically compared. Presumably these matters can be worked out, since Professor Ginter is already in touch with the Consortium about his plans.

The technical problems of recording and punching information on the division lists are not serious. On this point I can speak from experience since I have, for my own research, tabulated nearly 200 divisions, and found few difficulties. The kind of problem that occurs is, for example, differentiating between men of similar names who were recorded in the same way in the division lists, but these matters can generally be puzzled out, and relatively small numbers are involved in ambiguities of this character. It would be premature to discuss here matters of detail—how far, for example, the ten voting categories set up by the Consortium for the United States, or some adaptation of them, can be used for Great Britain—but the formats and procedures already worked out by the Consortium for handling roll calls might certainly be expected to provide at least some hints and guidelines when the time comes to tabulate divisions in the House of Commons.

I have tried to make some estimate of the size of the task. The division lists for 1836—1897 in the library of the Institute of Historical Research include 14,824 divisions, according to the count I have made. The divisions in Hansard from 1898 to 25 November 1966 amount to 19,839. This produces a total of 34,663. (The numbers of divisions for each year are shown in Table III.) Even if the divisions in Hansard for 1830—35 were added, the total would be only slightly over 35,000. This is a much smaller enterprise than that proposed by the Consortium for the United States. Though the exact figure is not yet known, the best present estimate appears to be that the Consortium will record, for both houses of Congress, from 1775 to the present, in the neighborhood of 60,000 roll calls. This is, of course, for a period about sixty years longer than that suggested for Great Britain, and for two houses and not one. This last point raises the question of the divisions in the House of

TABLE III

Number of Divisions in House of Commons Each Year, 1836—1966

Year	Number of Divisions	Year	Number of Divisions
1836	187	1867—68	168
1837	185	1868—69	160
1837—38	294	1870	244
1839	250	1871	270
1840	256	1872	287
1841 Session 1	109	1873	226
1841 Session 2	12	1874	162
1842	237	1875	248
1843	220	1876	242
1844	156	1877	314
1845	170	1878	278
1846	106	1878—79	237
1847	128	1880 Session 1	47
1847—48	255	1880 Session 2	169
1849	219	1881	411
1850	329	1882	405
1851	242	1883	314
1852	127	1884	216
1852—53	257	1884—85	289
1854	240	1886 Session 1	143
1854—55	213	1886 Session 2	46
1856	197	1887	485
1857 Session 1	15	1888	357
1857 Session 2	162	1889	360
1857—58	185	1890	262
1859 Session 1	41	1890—91	416
1859 Session 2	59	1892 Session 1	196
1860	265	1892 Session 2	1
1861	187	1893—94	450
1862	222	1894	246
1863	188	1895 Session 1	140
1864	156	1895 Session 2	38
1865	104	1896	413
1866	80	1897	367
1867	164	Total, 1836—1897	14,824

Year	Number of Divisions	Year	Number of Divisions
1898	310	1932–33	311
1899 Session 1	363	1933–34	414
1899 Session 2	18	1934–35	308
1900 Session 1	290	1935–36	326
1900 Session 2	8	1936–37	322
1901	482	1937–38	329
1902	648	1938–39	308
1903	263	1939–40	70
1904	341	1940–41	21
1905	364	1941–42	24
1906	501	1942–43	29
1907	466	1943–44	45
1908	463	1944–45	22
1909	920	1945–46	294
1910	159	1946–47	383
1911	451	1947–48	278
1912	604	1948 (Sept. 14–Oct. 25)	10
1913	17	1948–49	310
1914	214	1950 (Mar.–Oct.)	65
1914–15	34	1950–51	170
1916	67	1951–52	245
1917	157	1952–53	227
1918	95	1953–54	230
1919	166	1954–55 (Nov.–May)	61
1920	460	1955–56	298
1921 Session 1	367	1956–57	180
1921 Session 2	1	1957–58	206
1922	272	1958–59	177
1923	345	1959–60	156
1924	201	1960–61	269
1924–25	506	1961–62	261
1926	563	1962–63	183
1927	482	1963–64	148
1928	366	1964–65	276
1928–29	300	1965–66 (Nov.–Mar.)	39
1929–30	484	1966–67 (to Nov. 25, 1966	209
1930–31	521	Total, 1898–1966	19,839
1931–32	366	Grand Total	34,663

Lords, which will be discussed presently. It seems clear, however, that, for the House of Commons at least, the task suggested for Great Britain would be decidedly less than what is being attempted for the United States. The Consortium hopes to add data for future Congresses as well, and this would doubtless also be possible for Great Britain.

The most serious problem in the use of data on the division lists is neither the accessibility of the information nor its bulk, but something entirely different. The problem is the astonishingly low level of participation in voting in the House of Commons until quite recent times. The largest division on record is said to be that of 11 August 1892 when, on a motion expressing lack of confidence in the government, the vote was 350—310.[16] The size of the House at that time was 670, so that participation in this division was extremely high, even higher if one counts the four tellers. Such a pattern was, however altogether exceptional, as appears from Table IV, which gives figures on participation every tenth year from 1836 to the present. (I have used the year 1964—65 instead of 1965—66 since the information available to me for 1965—66 was not complete.) If the decennial samples in this table are a reliable guide, and the consistency of the figures suggests that some confidence may be placed in them, participation was extremely low until the twentieth century. The proportion of divisions in which at least 300 men participated, in a House that was always well over 600, appears to have been under one-tenth until the end of the 1850's, and well under one-half until the end of the nineteenth century. In the twentieth century, except in time of war, participation was greater, though still far from approaching completeness. For the division lists, as for electoral data, the difficulty is not to get the information but, rather, that much of the information one would like to have—the opinions of many members of parliament on many subjects—does not exist, since the events that would have produced it did not occur.

This brings up an issue of policy. The question may legitimately be raised to what extent these very small divisions, which are particularly numerous in the earlier period, are worth the trouble of tabulating. The purpose of recording votes in the divisions is presumably to provide information about the opinions of members of parliament on issues of the day. These tiny divisions, however, reveal the opinions of only a few men, and are not of much help in judging the temper of parliament as a whole. They also impose a restriction on the correla-

TABLE IV

Extent of Participation in Voting in Divisions in the House of Commons Since 1836

(The figures in the last four columns show, for each year, as a percentage, the proportion of divisions in which the number indicated at the top of the column participated. Thus, in 1836, the proportion of the divisions in which less than 100 men participated was 36.9%. In 1964–65, this proportion was 1.1%.)

Year	Total number of divisions	Extent of Participation in Voting			
		Under 100	100–199	200–299	300 or more
1836	187	36.9	43.3	11.8	8.0
1846	106	41.5	32.1	17.0	9.4
1856	197	14.2	46.7	30.0	9.1
1866	80	28.8	26.2	10.0	35.0
1876	242	16.5	29.8	30.2	23.5
1886	189	4.8	25.9	39.1	30.2
1896	413	0.2	21.8	37.3	40.7
1906	501	0.0	4.8	20.2	75.0
1916	67	16.4	46.3	32.8	4.5
1926	563	0.4	5.1	27.0	67.5
1935–36	326	0.0	7.1	23.3	69.6
1945–46	294	0.0	2.7	18.0	79.3
1955–56	298	0.7	3.0	11.1	85.2
1964–65	276	1.1	3.2	17.4	78.3

tion of votes in parliament with other kinds of information, such as the personal circumstances of members of parliament or the kinds of constituencies they represented. One cannot make these comparisons for members who did not vote; and it is always an open question how far the emerging patterns can be used to characterize the entire body.

It might be asked, then, whether a certain number of divisions, those below a stipulated minimum size, might not be omitted from the tabulations. Certainly this would result in a considerable saving of labor. Certainly, also, scholars working alone, with limited resources of time and money, have often followed the policy of disregarding roll calls in which the turnout did not reach a certain proportion of the total membership of the legislative body, say 50 percent, or even 80 percent. In my own research on the House of Commons in the 1840's when participation was low, I shall probably examine less than one-fifth of the divisions that took place in the parliament I am studying, and shall make a disproportionately larger use of the big divisions than of the small ones. The Consortium is recording all roll calls regardless of the degree of turnout or the degree of unanimity, but on this point the American example may not be relevant since those dealing with American roll-call data, I have been told, are not faced with the problem of nonparticipation on anything like the same scale.

On the other hand, omitting divisions below a certain size might involve losing valuable information. Questions dealt with in such divisions may have an interest for modern scholars that they apparently did not have for contemporaries. In view of what came of these matters later, it is interesting to trace their early development. It is also useful to learn what kinds of legislation slipped through the House of Commons with few or no divisions. Further, a study of the small divisions can reveal which Members of Parliament were regular attenders and participants, and on what subjects. Besides, there were periods when divisions were small for special reasons, as they apparently were in wartime, to judge from the figures in the table for 1916; and it would be undesirable to lose these by the general application of a cutoff point. It is also relevant that the use of certain techniques of analysis that are now available, such as scaling, may enable the student to extract more information from the small divisions than originally appeared possible.

For the most recent period of British history there is a problem of quite another kind. With the growth of party discipline, votes have tended more to follow party lines, and the division lists for the twentieth century, even though participation was high, may be of less value as indicators of opinion than those of the nineteenth century, when participation was low. There is a real question whether the division lists in the most recent period reveal enough additional information to be worth recording.

Here again, there is another side to the argument. Party discipline in the present age, though it is presumed to be strong, has not been checked by controlled observation, and it would be interesting to learn how far this impression is sustained by the facts. More important, we do not yet know when straight, or almost straight, party voting started. It is sometimes assumed to be a twentieth-century phenomenon but I have recently seen, in the research findings of some of my former students, evidence of strong correlation between party and vote in the second half of the nineteenth century.[17] On the other hand, there have been notorious deviations from straight party voting in the twentieth century. The story of the development of the relation between party and vote in the House of Commons is not yet known, and it is worth investigating.

There are also more general arguments for tabulating all divisions. A policy of comprehensiveness seems more justifiable for a permanent archive, to be used by different scholars for different purposes, than it would be for a project undertaken by a single individual. If all the data were included, individual scholars could, as they do with data from the Consortium, develop and use their own definitions of significance and exclude by mechanical means—an easy matter with the aid of computers—the classes of items they did not want. The policy of punching everything means also that complications of selection are avoided. If there is reasonable doubt about an item it may be better to include it than to exclude it, to avoid the trouble of having to retrace one's steps later. To cover everything while the machinery is in operation may be more economical of time in the long run. Further, a rigid commitment to a certain criterion may necessitate the exclusion of items that, in the light of further knowledge, one would want to keep. It is hard to lay down in advance a general rule that will cover all contingencies. If certain classes of items were omitted, one could never be sure how much distortion these omissions had produced. For these various reasons, the case for punching everything may be stronger than the case for attempting to make a selection.

Some thought should also be given to the possibility of recording divisions in the House of Lords as well. The situation here was very different. There were far fewer divisions, and the extent of participation, in relation to the total size of the House, was even less. Even for the nineteenth century there were relatively few divisions in which half the House participated and, in the decennial sample I have examined, there were none for the twentieth century. The House of Lords is one legislative body in which participation in voting has, over the last century, decreased instead of increasing, partly, no doubt, because of its enormous growth in size. It has more than doubled in the period since 1836, and has in fact doubled in the ninety years since 1876. The figures in Table V give some information about the number of divisions in the Lords and the size of the turnout. To get a rough estimate of the extent of this task, I have had a count made of the number of divisions in Hansard, taking one year in each decade from 1836 to 1966. For these fourteen dates there was a total of 216 divisions, an average of 15.43 divisions a year. This figure, extrapolated for the entire 131-year period, yields an estimate of 2,021 divisions. Though this estimate is extremely rough, it will serve to give a general idea of the amount of work involved. It seems clear that the addition of perhaps 2,000 divisions in the Lords to the 35,000 divisions in the Commons, making a total of 37,000 would not be an enterprise of great magnitude.

Whether it is worth doing is another question. One could not, for the Lords, as would be possible for the Commons, correlate political attitudes with electoral and demographic data, since members of the House of Lords were not elected and, though some of them had deep local roots, were not politically tied to certain constituencies as were members of the House of Commons. One could, however, work out patterns of political attitudes from the division lists, so far as the information reaches, and examine the correlations of these patterns with party membership. Also, votes in the House of Lords might be interesting on other grounds: in the nineteenth century, because of the still great power and influence of this house and the frequent location of party leadership there; in the twentieth century, because of the special tone of the House that has developed, in contrast with the Commons— the more leisurely and extended examination of issues in debate, and

TABLE V
Extent of Participation in Voting in the House of Lords Since 1836

Year	Total number of divisions	Size of divisions (proxies, when stated, included)					Total membership of House
		1–49	50–99	100–199	200–299	300–399	
1836	22	3	12	4	1	2	435
1846	3	1	0	0	1	1	459
1856	7	1	2	2	2	0	455
1866	12	2	8	2	0	0	460
1876	5	0	2	1	2	0	501
1886	7	0	1	4	2	0	544
1896	15	1	2	11	1	0	575
1906	38	1	4	26	7	0	613
1916	2	1	1	0	0	0	659
1926	30	3	15	11	1	0	720
1935–36	22	6	14	2	0	0	750
1945–46	10	0	10	0	0	0	810
1955–56	26	5	19	1	0	1	844
1965–66	17	2	9	6	0	0	1,013

the rather different configurations of parties and of other political groups. Though the divisions in the Lords are less important than those in the Commons, they are interesting in their own right; and it is possible that this relatively small addition to the total task might be well worth undertaking.

3 DEMOGRAPHIC DATA

Information on economic and social conditions in the constituencies is not always easy to get, but there can be little doubt about its theoretical interest in view of the accumulated findings showing its relation to the political attitudes of members of a legislature.[18] Some recent research has indeed suggested that demographic data may ultimately prove more significant than electoral data in the study of legislative behavior.[19] What has been discovered for the United States and other countries in the mid-twentieth century does not, of course, necessarily hold for Great Britain in the nineteenth century; but the questions that have been raised in some of the studies of the contemporary scene are so interesting and their implications so broad that it would be a pity not to investigate them, so far as this can be done, for earlier periods as well.

This discussion of demographic data can be only tentative, since I am not qualified as a demographer and have done little research that involves the use of the Census or similar materials. In planning this phase of the project it would be essential to seek the aid of those who have special experience with such matters: demographers, and social and economic historians. This is particularly desirable since the incorporation of demographic information will, as has been pointed out,[20] make the data archive of interest to a wider group than political historians, and those who will use it for other purposes should be consulted as to what kinds of data should be gathered.

The example of the Consortium is less helpful in this field than in the areas of electoral and roll-call data, since its program of collecting demographic data is still in a relatively early stage, and it is not yet clear what categories of data it will be able to process. I have been referred, for general guidance, to the report of a conference on historical demographic data held at the University of Pennsylvania on October 16, 1964, which recommended the tabulation of eleven classes of information.[21] I have used these eleven categories, plus five others kindly furnished me by the Director of Data Recovery at the Consortium, to make some preliminary comparisons.

It might be interesting, as a tentative first step, to see how far such material can be found in the reports of the British Census. The pamphlet describing the British Census from 1801 to 1931, which is one of the *Guides to Official Sources* published by H.M. Stationery Office,[22] can serve as a general guide for this trial run.

Table VI shows to what extent information on each of the sixteen categories, or the nearest thing to it, is listed as available for Great Britain. I have reason to suppose that the table does not tell the whole story since I have found, in looking over individual Census reports for different dates, considerably more material than is here indicated. Yet Table VI, however incomplete it may be, suggests that information for Great Britain can be obtained on a substantial number of the points on which the Consortium is considering collecting information for the United States, though not for all years and not always quite the same information. There is at least something to show for ten of the sixteen categories.

Also, a number of the gaps can probably be easily filled in. Figures can be found at various points in the *Parliamentary Papers* on the area of constituencies[23] and on the numbers of illiterates at elections,[24] #4 and #12. In regard to the value of land and buildings, #9, Dod's *Parliamentary Companion*, until 1885, gives for each constituency the "Number of 10£ Houses" and McCalmont's *Parliamentary Poll Book* gives a figure for the value of "Property." On industrial and agricultural production, #10 and #15, Mitchell and Deane give gross national figures and, sometimes, regional figures. It may be possible to extract further information from the handbooks, from *Parliamentary Papers*, from local histories,[25] or from local guides and directories.

Yet the collection of such materials, even on a national basis, may not be easy. The British Census was, in the early nineteenth century, a beginning enterprise. Although the first United States Census was taken in 1790, the first for Britain was in 1801 and the first for Ireland in 1821. In Britain, as in the United States, the Census inquiries changed in scope, so that certain types of information are available only for a restricted number of years. On the whole the early Census reports are less complete and, for some classes of data, there is adequate information only from the middle or from the end of the nineteenth century. There may be similar problems with other sources; I have noticed that many of the time series in Mitchell and Deane start late and do not cover the whole nineteenth century. There have also occurred, in successive Census reports, changes in definition and in methods of classification, to such an extent that, for some important categories such as occupation, it is hard to get comparable figures for any extended period.[26]

The greatest difficulty, however, appears to be that of getting demographic information at the constituency level, the form in which it would be most useful for the study of political history. Even on the elementary point of population, the figures in the Census may not yield everything that is needed.[27] For other kinds of information the task may be even more formidable, in view of the variety of local jurisdictions. The subdivisions of Britain used for ecclesiastical purposes, local government, parliamentary representation, the administration of justice, and the registration of births, deaths, and marriages differed from one another to such an extent as to bring the compilers of the Census to a state of frustration. In the general report of the 1901 Census for England and Wales there appears the following statement: "The whole of England and Wales has been divided at different times into various administrative areas with so little regard for previously existing divisions that, at the present time, the serious overlappings of boundaries render the work both of the Census Office and local Officials, in ascertaining the precise limits of the several divisions to be separately distinguished in the Tables, laborious and extremely complicated."[28] These difficulties are heightened, of course, by the fact that the boundaries of parliamentary constituencies were altered by legislation at various times during the nineteenth and twentieth centuries.

The past failure of the Census to provide information on a constituency basis apparently constitutes a major impediment to the kind of research envisaged in this paper. I am not sufficiently experienced to estimate the extent of this difficulty, but I have consulted those better informed and find that, for the most part, they tend to take a pessimistic view. I have also been told that there seems no way of obtaining this information retrospectively and that the ingenious efforts to get around this problem by various means have not proved entirely adequate. Though the first and second parts of the project seem quite feasible for England, the collection of demographic data in a form useful for politi-

TABLE VI
Demographic Information

Points on which the Consortium is considering collecting information for the United States	Years for which information on these subjects or on related matters is available from the British Census
1. Nativity	Birthplace and nationality,
2. Race	1841—
3. Religion	1851 only
4. Area—square miles	
5. Total population	1801—
6. Age distribution	1821, 1841—
7. Sex	1801—
8. Percentage urban, in different sized categories	
9. Value of land and buildings, both rural and urban	
10. Value of manufactured products	
11. Occupation	Personal occupation, 1801, 1841— Family occupation, 1811—1831 Whether employer or employed, 1841—
12. Literacy rates	
13. School attendance	1851—1921, but apparently not for 1931; in 1891 and 1901 for Scotland only
14. Family size	Condition as to marriage, 1851— Children of present marriage, 1911 Number of children under 16, 1921
15. Agricultural production (general categories rather than specific commodities)	
16. Home and farm ownership and indebtedness	Number of houses inhabited, 1801— How many families occupying house, 1801—1831, 1911—1931 Houses being built, 1811—1921; not 1931 Houses uninhabited, 1801— Number of rooms in household, 1891—(England and Wales only)

cal analysis presents considerable difficulties. It may turn out that this part of the project, if it is carried through, can be handled only in a less precise and less satisfactory manner.

If demographic data can be incorporated, however, there is certainly a great deal of it, and its richness and diversity will make necessary some difficult decisions about what classes of information should be included or excluded, and what arrangements of the information will be most useful for research purposes. I understand from my friends at the Consortium that they anticipate that demographic data may present more severe processing problems than will either of the other two types of material: that the large and varied body of demographic data available for the United States makes the choice of categories a complicated one, that the bulk of the material it will probably be necessary to handle is expected to be enormous, and that the number of variables involved will present serious technical problems. Similar difficulties can probably be expected for Great Britain.

In any case, this phase of the enterprise, if it proves feasible, would clearly depend far more than the other two upon the cooperation of British scholars. A good deal of the work on electoral and roll-call data could be done in the United States. For demographic information it would be necessary to rely much more on sources available only in Britain. Help will be needed from scholars there, not only for supervising the work, but also for planning it, and for deciding what categories of materials should be assembled.

4 CONCLUSIONS

It seems clear, then, that for electoral and roll-call data there exists, for Great Britain in the nineteenth and twentieth centuries, a large body of relevant and useful information which is readily accessible in a form convenient for tabulating. The record is probably less complete for Britain than for the United States because of the frequency of uncontested elections and the relatively low rate of participation in divisions until recent times, as well as the absence of official published division lists until 1836; yet, despite this, the materials available on both elections and divisions are still enormous, and no doubt sufficiently informative to be well worth recording. It does not appear that the size of the job would be a major obstacle since, for these two types of data at least, the task is smaller for Great Britain than for the United States: one type of election as compared with four, and 37,000 roll calls as compared with 60,000.

For demographic materials the situation is less clear and it is not possible to speak with so much assurance. There is reason to suppose that much information is available that would be of great value for political history. What is not certain is how much information it will be possible to get on a constituency basis. This may prove a real stumbling block, and on this point parallel studies between Great Britain and the United States may be more difficult.

There is also a technical problem which need not be discussed at length here, but which should be identified so that it will not be lost from sight. If the collected materials are to be made available in machine-readable form to scholars both in Great Britain and the United States, special arrangements will be necessitated since, to a considerable degree, different kinds of machines are in use in the two countries. It will be necessary to settle at the outset on policies for the transferral of information so that data recorded in one country can immediately be put on cards or tape usable in the other. The details will have to be worked out by specialists in computer work who are acquainted with the procedures in both countries. I have been told by those who know more about these matters than I do that the problem, though it may be troublesome, is by no means insurmountable.

The special interest of the data collection project described in this paper is that it relates closely to two major and to some extent connected phases of present-day scholarship: the extensive interest in parliamentary history that has developed over the last several decades, and the active contemporary experimentation with quantitative methods in the study of political history. For the history of parliament this project would make a distinctive contribution of a kind that has not yet, at least on this scale, been attempted. For quantitative research it would provide a body of basic and important data that would serve, if the American experience can be taken as a guide, as an effective aid and stimulus.

One of the most considerable results of the recent concern with parliamentary history has been the setting up of the History of Parliament Trust, which operates under an annual grant placed at its disposal by the British Government in 1951.[29] Its program is an immense one, comparable in bulk to that of the Consortium, though in other respects these are very dissimilar enterprises. The Trust is undertaking to publish biographies of all men who sat in the House of Commons up to 1901, together with certain other information about the history of parliament. The first installment, the impressive three volumes covering the period 1754–1790, by Sir Lewis Namier and John Brooke, appeared in 1964, and the next set of volumes, by Romney Sedgwick, covering the period 1715–1754, is expected to appear shortly. The *History of Parliament* will present not only biographies of individuals, which of course is not a part of the Consortium's program, but also certain other information more closely related to the concerns of the Consortium. I am informed that it is intended, so far as the evidence permits, to state how many votes were cast for individual candidates at contested elections, to describe the voting records of Members of Parliament, and to say something about the political structure and behavior of constituencies at different times.

This sounds, at first, sufficiently like the program proposed here as to raise the question of duplication of effort. If there is any likelihood of this, the present project should not be attempted. Every effort should be made to leave the Trust a clear field in the area that it has marked out for itself. I believe, however, that the two enterprises are entirely different, and that no problem of duplication may be expected to arise.

The Trust, so far as I am informed, does not propose to set up a data archive. The information it collects will be stored in books and not in machines. The difference is not a trivial one. For the kind of research that has been assumed as an objective throughout this paper, which requires the manipulation and comparison of large amounts of different kinds of data, it is essential that the data be "so ordered and stored as to be retrievable in almost any subset or combination of subsets." Furthermore, the exceptionally rich possibilities for such research "can be realized only through the use of a high-speed computer for storage, retrieval, and data processing."[30] To present in book form all the information that could be stored and used in this way would be an unprofitable undertaking for the Trust or for anyone else. A given individual sitting in parliament in the nineteenth or the twentieth century might have the opportunity to vote in several thousand divisions. To publish his votes or abstentions in all of these, and to do the same for every other individual in parliament, would be an inefficient use of space. Such information is too voluminous and, by itself, too unimportant to be worth printing, although if punched on cards and manipulated by machines it can be used for research in a constructive fashion. Even if all these materials were printed they would eventually, to make it possible to work with them effectively, have to be put on cards or tape. To proceed otherwise, in the present state of research techniques, would involve a waste of time that could only be described as calamitous. For electoral data similar considerations apply. It would be possible to gather and print the votes for individual candidates in each contested election but, if correlations and other work with these materials were to be attempted on any extensive scale, the matter could not be left there: it would be necessary to punch the information as well. The same argument applies to demographic information, with which, by the way, I gather that the Trust is less concerned.

This project would, then, be supplementary to the work of the Trust and would make a contribution to parliamentary history of a different kind. There seems no serious danger of an overlap, even when the work of the Trust is extended into the nineteenth century, as I hope it eventually will be. It seems highly desirable, on the other hand, that the officials of the History of Parliament Trust be consulted and kept informed in regard to plans, and that full use be made of any cooperation that they are willing to provide. Their experience and knowledge could be of great assistance for this project, and it is fortunate that they have already expressed a benevolent interest in it.

For historians interested in quantitative research, the number of whom seems to be fast increasing,[31] an archive of basic political data would have great value. Research of this kind, when an individual is working alone, requires much intensive and uninteresting labor at the outset. It takes a long time before the preliminary tasks are completed and the results begin to show, as I have learned from my own experience. The ready accessibility of the necessary information, or a substantial amount of it, would make a great difference. The availability of such data changes the character of the research problem: it is no longer a matter of trying to reach the stage where the materials have been gathered; one can take this as a starting point and go on from there. A collection of data in this form would greatly facilitate the work of scholars now engaged in such studies, as well as making further such enterprises possible, or much more feasible than they would be in present circumstances.

The value of quantitative research is, of course, still debated in some quarters. I have said elsewhere what I have to say on the subject,[32] and need not repeat myself here. It may be enough to point out that, though the published studies are unequal in value, it seems clear already that substantial results have been achieved. Accepted theories have been refuted, former assumptions about the character of the representative process have been called into question, general issues have been clarified and their discussion placed on a firmer basis, and new and interesting questions have been raised. The accomplishments along this line are already so considerable, the lines of inquiry that have been opened up are so promising, and the interest of scholars is so active that a good case can be made for supporting this work on a considerable scale.

Such a project would not only serve present research but would also be guided by it and, in this manner, benefit from it. Those in charge of collecting quantitative data on modern British political history would not be flying blind. They would, on the contrary, have excellent indications as to the kinds of materials it would be most useful to gather and the purposes they could serve. The study of representative institutions in Britain and America has raised questions on which these materials would bear and, in so doing, has laid out some fairly clear paths for the assembling of further information. The two great data-collection programs in the two countries, though neither would duplicate this effort, could furnish guidance for it. The History of Parliament Trust, though its labors are directed to a somewhat different purpose, could provide background and assistance. The work of the Consortium, though its example should not be slavishly followed, can still serve in certain important respects as a precedent.

These data would enable historians to study, with more convenience and more precision, the general trends in each of these three subject areas: the changes in the patterns of electoral behavior and the strength of the various party groups at different times in different kinds of constituencies; the patterns of voting in parliament and what they reveal about the thinking of contemporaries on the subjects under consideration, as well as the relation, at different times, of votes to party affiliation;[33] and finally, if it proves feasible to handle demographic data, the kinds of demographic conditions prevailing in different types

of constituencies. Even more interesting would be the correlation of
these three kinds of information together: the study of the relation
of demographic conditions to what happened in the elections, making due allowance for the "ecological fallacy",[34] and the study of the
relation of both these variables to the political attitudes and behavior
of members of parliament. These points could be further elaborated but
perhaps enough has been said to indicate that, with proper materials
and proper tools to use them, it might be possible to raise some fairly
basic questions about the nature of legislative behavior and the motives
of political action, and to achieve some clarification of these subjects,
limiting the number of hypotheses that could be considered, and placing the discussion on a more solid foundation.

NOTES

1. This paper was prepared for a meeting of the American Historical Association's Committee on Quantitative Data at Ann Arbor, Michigan, November
   10–11, 1967. I wish to express my thanks to William J. Marland, my
   research assistant, for help in assembling these materials and to Jerome
   M. Clubb, Director of Data Recovery at the Inter-University Consortium
   for Political Research, for providing me with information about the
   operation and plans of the Consortium. I am indebted also to colleagues
   both in the United States and in England who have read the paper and
   have made a number of extremely useful suggestions.

2. Inter-University Consortium for Political Research, *Annual Report, 1964–
   1965*, p. 13.

3. Economic history is the basic emphasis of the indispensable collection
   of materials assembled by B. R. Mitchell and Phyllis Deane, while quantitative materials have been used for social history with impressive results
   by, among others, Lawrence Stone, Peter Laslett, E. A. Wrigley, and R. S.
   Schofield.

4. See, for further details on local elections, David Butler and Jennie Freeman,
   British Political Facts, 1900–1960 (London, 1963), pp. 189, 192–193.

5. Consortium, *Annual Report, 1964–1965*, p. 15.

6. In addition to the information in the Parliamentary or Sessional Papers,
   convenient summaries of election figures can be found in a variety of
   readily accessible handbooks or similar sources. For the nineteenth century
   there are the successive volumes of Dod's *Parliamentary Companion*, Dod's

Electoral Facts . . . (2nd ed., London, 1853) which covers the years 1832–
1852, McCalmont's *Parliamentary Poll Book,* and *The Times* and other newspapers. Some information can also be gleaned from the *Annual Register*
and Whitaker's *Almanac.* For the twentieth century, and especially for the
most recent period, the convenient secondary sources are even more
ample. B. R. Mitchell and Klaus Boehm present detailed figures for the
five elections in the years 1950–1964 in *British Parliamentary Election
Results, 1950–1964* (Cambridge, England, 1966). They used as sources,
besides the material in the Sessional Papers, the successive books of *The
House of Commons* published after each general election by *The Times,* and
also the Press Association *List of Candidates* which was made available to
them by the Press Association, Ltd. Further sources for electoral data are
listed in Butler and Freeman, *British Political Facts,* p. 131.

7. D. C. Moore, "Social Structure, Political Structure, and Public Opinion in
Mid-Victorian England," in R. Robson, ed., *Ideas and Institutions of Victorian
Britain: Essays in Honour of George Kitson Clark* (London, 1967), pp. 20–57;
J. R. Vincent, *Pollbooks: How Victorians Voted* (Cambridge, England, 1967).

8. H. J. Hanham, *Elections and Party Management: Politics in the Time of Disraeli
and Gladstone* (London, 1959), p. 199. See also Trevor Lloyd, "Uncontested
Seats in British General Elections, 1852–1910," *Historical Journal,* **VII**,
2 (1965), pp. 260–265.

9. Norman Gash, *Politics in the Age of Peel: A Study in the Technique of Parliamentary Representation, 1830–1850* (London, etc., 1953), p. 440.

10. The figures in Table I are based principally on the following sources:
Returns of Election Expenses in *Parliamentary Papers;* the successive volumes
of Dod's *Parliamentary Companion;* Dod's *Electoral Facts . . .* (2nd ed., London,
1853); F. H. McCalmont, *The Parliamentary Poll Book of All Elections from the
Reform Act of 1832 to February, 1910 (Inclusive) . . .* (7th ed., London and
Nottingham, 1910); and *The Times.* The incidence of election contests for
various parts of this period has been discussed by Trevor Lloyd, H. J.
Hanham, and Norman Gash in the publications already cited. It has also
been dealt with by James Frederick Stanley Ross in *Elections and Electors:
Studies in Democratic Representation* (London, 1955). Gash's figures are for
uncontested constituencies, not uncontested seats. The figures in Table I
do not always exactly agree with those presented by the other writers, but
I prefer to keep my own figures, at least until I have seen evidence that they
need to be changed. Most of the discrepancies are, in any case, small. A
special problem in calculating the proportion of uncontested seats
in each election is that there were slight changes from time to time in the
size of the House of Commons. Sudbury (2 seats) was disfranchised in 1844,

reducing the number of seats in 1847 to 656, and St. Albans (2 seats) was disfranchised in 1852, so that only 654 seats were available in the elections of 1852, 1857 and 1859; these four seats were reassigned in 1861. Lancaster (2 seats), Reigate (1), Totnes (2) and Great Yarmouth (2) were disfranchised in 1867, but their seats were reassigned for the general election of 1868 and their disfranchisement does not affect the figures. Beverly (2 seats), Bridge-water (2), Cashel (1) and Sligo (1) were disfranchised in 1870, which reduces to 652 the number of seats in 1874 and 1880, the two elections between 1870 and the general redistribution of 1885.

11. Hanham, *Op. cit.*, pp. 191, 197–198.

12. Hanham, *Op. cit.*, pp. 191–192.

13. "Election figures suffer much more from being inherently confusing than from being inaccurately reported. The complications that arise from unopposed returns, from plural voting, from two-member seats, and, above all, from variations in the number of candidates put up by each party, are the really serious hazards in psephological interpretation." (Butler and Freeman, *British Political Facts*, p. 121.) Some of these problems have also been discussed by other writers. See especially Henry Pelling's *Social Geography of British Elections, 1885–1910* (London, etc., 1967).

14. A. Lawrence Lowell, "The Influence of Party Upon Legislation in England and America," *Annual Report of the American Historical Association for the Year 1901* (Washington, 1902), I, pp. 321–542.

15. The published division lists, however, though they give the names of the tellers, do not list the pairs; for these it is necessary to go to Hansard.

16. Norman Wilding and Philip Laundy, *An Encyclopaedia of Parliament* (London, 1958), p. 154.

17. John Robert Bylsma, *Political Issues and Party Unity in the House of Commons, 1852–1857: A Scalogram Analysis* (Ph.D. Dissertation, University of Iowa, 1968); James Cook Hamilton, *Parties and Voting Patterns in the Parliament of 1874–1880* (Ph.D. Dissertation, University of Iowa, 1968).

18. This appears, for the twentieth century, in a variety of studies. I have presented some evidence for the mid-nineteenth century on the subject in "The Country Gentlemen and the Repeal of the Corn Laws," *English Historical Review*, **LXXXII** (January 1967), pp. 54–55, 60.

19. A number of these findings, and the challenges to accepted views that they present, have been discussed by John C. Wahlke in an unpublished paper, "Public Policy and Representative Government: the Role of the Represented," presented at the Seventh World Congress of the Inter-

national Political Science Association in Brussels, September 1967; pp. 26–29.

20. Report by Samuel P. Hays on the conference on historical demographic data on October 16, 1964, Consortium, *Annual Report, 1964–1965*, p. 34.

21. *Ibid.*, p. 36.

22. *Census Reports of Great Britain, 1801–1931. (Inter-departmental Committee on Social and Economic Research, Guides to Official Sources, No. 2)* (London, 1931).

23. For example, in *Parliamentary Papers*, 1883, **54**, pp. 369ff.

24. *Return of Number of Illiterates at Elections in the United Kingdom* published at various dates including, for example, 1890–91, 1892, 1893–94, 1896.

25. Charles Gross's famous bibliography of local history, now over seventy years old, has recently been revised and brought up to date. Charles Gross, *A Bibliography of British Municipal History, Including Gilds and Parliamentary Representation*, 2nd ed., with a preface by G. H. Martin (Leicester University Press, 1966). The first volume of a supplementary work, *A Bibliography of British and Irish Municipal History* by G. H. Martin and Sylvia MacIntyre, will be published by the Leicester University Press in 1971.

26. The difficulties and hazards of using Census data, particularly for the early part of the nineteenth century, have been more extensively discussed by G. Kitson Clark in *The Critical Historian* (New York, 1967), pp. 182ff.

27. The populations of parliamentary cities, boroughs, and districts of boroughs in England and Wales were first given in 1841, the addition of this information apparently being considered necessary after the reform legislation of 1832 had destroyed the identity between municipal and parliamentary boroughs that had hitherto existed. It was not until 1851, however, that population figures were given for the 21 burghs and districts of burghs in Scotland entitled to send members to parliament, or for parliamentary counties and parliamentary county divisions. (*Census Reports of Great Britain, 1801–1931*, pp. 7, 98–101.)

28. *Census Reports of Great Britain, 1801–1931*, p. 95.

29. I wish to thank E. L. C. Mullins, the Secretary to the Editorial Board of the History of Parliament Trust, for supplying me with certain information about the operations and plans of the Trust.

30. Consortium, *Annual Report, 1964–1965*, pp. 14–15.

31. For recent summaries see Allan G. Bogue, "United States: the 'New'

Political History," *Journal of Contemporary History*, **3**, 1 (January 1968), pp. 5—27; Samuel P. Hays, "Computers and Historical Research," in Edmund A. Bowles, ed., *Computers in Humanistic Research: Readings and Perspectives* (Englewood Cliffs, N. J., 1967); Robert P. Swierenga, "Clio and Computers: A Survey of Computerized Research in History," *Computers and the Humanities*, **5**, 1 (September, 1970), pp. 1—21.

32. "Quantification in History," *American Historical Review*, **LXXI**, 3 (April 1966), pp. 803—825, published as Chapter 2 in this volume.

33. I have tried to show how this could be done in "Voting Patterns in the British House of Commons in the 1840s," *Comparative Studies in Society and History*, **V**, 2 (January 1963), pp. 134—163; "Parties and Issues in Early Victorian England," *Journal of British Studies*, **V**, 2 (May 1966), pp. 95—114.

34. W. S. Robinson, "Ecological Correlations and the Behavior of Individuals," *American Sociological Review*, **15**, 3 (June 1950), pp. 351—357. See also Leo A. Goodman, "Some Alternatives to Ecological Correlation," *American Sociological Review*, **64**, 6 (May 1959), pp. 610—625.

CHAPTER 5

PROBLEMS OF METHOD IN A PARTICULAR CASE: THE PARLIAMENT OF 1841

During the last several years I have been working on a detailed statistical study of the 815 men who sat in the house of commons between the general elections of 1841 and 1847. The purpose of the research is to throw light on certain questions about the social and economic composition of the house and the political behavior of the various groups in it, questions which, though important and widely discussed, cannot, I find, be answered in the present state of our knowledge. The project, though it makes use only of elementary statistical techniques, is elaborate and, if it does not depart in principle from earlier historical ventures into statistics, it does perhaps depart from them in degree. I am incorporating a large amount of biographical data, tabulating votes in divisions in the house of commons as well as biographical facts, making correlations as well as counting aggregates, and using mechanical aids—punch-cards and I[nternational] B[usiness] M[achines]— to handle the information and to perform certain complicated tasks with it. I will not attempt to describe the project further, since I am publishing elsewhere[1] a detailed account of it and of some of the preliminary conclusions.

This paper will be devoted merely to a few problems of method that have come up in this research. I wish to say something about the earlier applications of statistics to historical study, to discuss briefly the possible uses of the method, and finally and most important to deal with the practical problems which this method presents. It is not easy to apply these rather rigid techniques to the slippery and evasive data of history. The fact that my research makes a relatively ambitious use of statistics has made me particularly aware of these difficulties, and there may be some value in an exposition of them by one who has attempted even in a limited field correlations of some complexity. Though I believe the method has, at least for the area in which I am working, great advantages, I am also in a position to testify that its limitations of scope are significant and that its technical difficulties are formidable.

That insight into the character of a representative body or any other body of men may be obtained from a biographical analysis of its individual members, and that the results of such a survey may be most readily grasped by counting them, by a quantitative method, are principles that have been for some time accepted and acted upon by an important group of historians. The comparative biographical analysis of a limited group was a technique applied by Professor Beard, as early as 1913, to the founding fathers, with results that were important and stimulating in the highest degree.[2] During the last twenty-five years this approach, in the hands of Sir Lewis Namier and other historians, has become the basis of perhaps the most important new departure in historical method of our time.[3] As examples of the application of the technique to nonparliamentary bodies one might cite Professor Crane Brinton's monumental statistical survey of the Jacobins published in 1930,[4] and Professor Donald M. Greer's two illuminating statistical monographs on the victims of the Terror and on the *emigrés* during the French Revolution.[5] A recent application of the method is Mr. William Miller's series of essays on American business executives in the early twentieth century.[6] On a smaller scale, in a number of scattered articles or short essays, historians have applied statistics to businessmen,[7] cabinet officers,[8] ambassadors and diplomats,[9] Nazi Party members,[10] and other groups.[11]

Foreshadowings of the method can be found earlier. Over a century ago Bernard Cracroft published, in his contribution to *Essays on Reform*, a suggestive account of the economic interests and social groups in the last house of commons elected before the Reform Bill of 1867.[12] His essay anticipated later trends in scholarship by many years, and modern students of the history of parliament can still gain something from it. Going still further back, one can find at least an adumbration of the method in Burke's famous diatribe against the National Assembly:[13]

This unforced choice, this fond election of evil, would appear perfectly un-accountable if we did not consider the composition of the national assembly: I do not mean its formal constitution, which as it now stands is exceptionable enough, but the materials of which, in a great measure, it is composed, which is of ten thousand times greater consequence than all the formalities in the world . . .

After I had read over the list of the persons and descriptions selected into the *Tiers Etat*, nothing which they afterwards did could appear astonishing . . .

Judge, sir, of my surprise, when I found that a very great proportion of the assembly (a majority, I believe, of the members who attended) was com-posed of practitioners in the law . . . From the moment I read the list, I saw distinctly, and very nearly as it has happened, all that was to follow.

Jefferson in his *Autobiography* made a remark on the composition of Congress which may be quoted in the same context:[14]

If the present Congress errs in too much talking, how can it be otherwise, in a body to which the people send one hundred and fifty lawyers, whose trade is to question everything, yield nothing, and talk by the hour? That one hundred and fifty lawyers should do business together, ought not to be expected.

These judgments are unqualified and presuppose a more simple relationship of cause and effect than a modern historian would care to admit. Yet both statements contain in unmistakable form the germ of the idea that the political actions of a group can be better understood through a composite, quantitative account of the backgrounds of its members.

To these quotations should be added one more. I was pleased to dis-cover, when rereading Boswell a couple of years ago, the following brief conversation, which my current interest in statistics invested with a new significance.[15]

BOSWELL. Sir Alexander Dick tells me, that he remembers having a thousand people in a year to dine at his house: that is, reckoning each person as one, each time that he dined there.

JOHNSON. That, Sir, is about three a day.

BOSWELL. How your statement lessens the idea.

JOHNSON. That, Sir, is the good of counting. It brings everything to a certainty, which before floated in the mind indefinitely.

The principle of the statistical method is at base nothing more than this, and the case for it could scarcely be stated more cogently. Dr. Johnson's trenchant comment is the more welcome because it helps to clear away the mystification vulgarly attached to statistics. In essence the method is a very simple thing: the arrangement in a convenient order of similar facts which are so numerous that, without such arrangement, their general purport could not be readily grasped. In other words, it serves to substitute an exact statement for a general impression. General impressions, though historians sometimes cling to them affectionately, are notoriously misleading. Even when they are based on considerable knowledge they may contain biases and preconceptions of which the writer is unaware. It is a common experience that facts which fit a previously formed theory or opinion strike the imagination more forcibly and are more easily remembered. A quantitative method helps the historian to escape from the catch phrases and legends that have been built up about the past, to avoid imposing upon it contemporary patterns of thought, and to emancipate himself from his own preconceptions.

Statistics will, of course, occasionally confirm traditional views, for it is not to be expected that the careful work of generations of historians will be overturned all in a moment. Indeed the method is little more than the exercise of common sense and judgment upon quantitative data, and many historians who never set up their findings in the form of tables have nevertheless used at least a rudimentary statistical approach. The confirmation of a traditional view is, in any case, itself a discovery for it enables us, not only to express with greater certainty what could previously be merely surmised, but also to describe with measurable precision what could previously be stated only in general terms. Furthermore when, as often happens in a complex field of study, the existing interpretations disagree, a quantitative analysis will make it possible to choose between them or, if neither proves correct, to test alternative hypotheses set up in accordance with what appears to be the trend of the evidence.

The excursions of historians into statistics are all interesting and some, the work, for example, of Professor Beard or of Sir Lewis Namier, have been epoch-making. The method can no longer be spoken of as a novelty of dubious value. Its usefulness is not only, as one would suppose, self-evident, but has also been amply demonstrated in several profoundly significant historical studies.

It is curious, then, that it has not been more widely adopted. Unquestionably the classic historical techniques of verification have been directed more to individual facts or events than to the broad developments of social or political history, the general or usual behavior of groups composed of large numbers of individuals. Professor Hofstadter has called attention to the loss to American historical understanding caused by the reluctance of men of Beard's generation to seize upon and apply Beard's remarkable innovations in technique. "Historical writing today . . . is still wanting in method, in no small part because of a curious failure to explore the vistas opened by Beard thirty-seven years ago".[16] In my own field of research, English history in the nineteenth century, the dearth of quantitative studies has led to strange disagreements on some of the fundamental historical issues of the period, issues on which one would expect that precise statements could be made. At present it is simply not possible to state the accepted position on such important matters as the degree of the infiltration of businessmen into parliament by the 1840's, the extent to which the gentry in parliament were active in business, the extent to which businessmen in parliament had married into the gentry, the political attitudes (as shown by party membership and by votes on major legislation) of the various social and economic groups in parliament, and even the attitudes of the different parties on issues that cut across party lines. The period is so complex that the evidence on these questions points both ways, and some support can be found for almost any thesis. On many of these questions different and contradictory opinions can be found, each buttressed by enough evidence to make a plausible case.

The lack of interest in quantitative techniques has also had the result that the method has not been developed and refined over the past several decades, as would presumably have happened if a larger number of historians had been giving some attention to it. Despite the immense importance of what has been done, historians have barely grazed the surface in the application of this powerful instrument to their own problems. Not only could a far larger amount of data be submitted to formal statistical treatment, but much more could also be done in the correlation of different kinds of data. Although there are a few exceptions, historians using statistics have dealt with aggregates rather than with statistical relationships, or have attempted correlations only of the simplest kind. Yet a correlation of different types of information with each other, social background with economic interest, or either with votes, leads at once to results that are on an entirely new level of interest.

Whatever may be the reason for this failure to exploit statistical techniques, it must be admitted that the method is not easy to apply. Its problems might be conveniently grouped under three headings, in ascending order of difficulty: the manual labor; the availability of the evidence or the problems of research; and the similarity of the evidence or the problems of classification. These problems might well occasion serious reservations about the appropriateness of statistics for historical research, and to some extent I share such reservations, as the following argument will show. The issue seems to be, however, not the usefulness of the method, for it is always useful to arrange one's materials in an orderly fashion, but its feasibility. It is to this question that the following remarks are addressed.

The first of the three problems is the most easily disposed of. The problem is that, for a statistical study that goes to any depth, an immense bulk of information is required, and a difficulty which develops almost at the outset is how to put these data in a form in which they can be manipulated. The sheer nuisance of handling the materials is undoubtedly a major deterrent to the use of the method. Fortunately there lie ready to hand technical devices that have been developed in other fields. Work of the complexity that is required if the method is to be extended to historical problems on a large scale could probably not be undertaken without the use of mechanical aids, Hollerith cards, and IBM machines. Though some historians regard these contraptions with disfavor, it is difficult to see how the use of them can be avoided if the statistical weapon is to be employed at more than a fraction of its potential strength. Perhaps the rôle of these machines in research is not always understood. The fact that I make use of them has attracted a disproportionate amount of attention from some of my colleagues. A few even seem to regard these mechanical paraphernalia as the first step in the domination of the profession by robots and the ultimate technological unemployment of historians. The impression seems to be that this technique implies the abandonment of the historian's reasoning powers and the entrusting of the task of thinking out historical problems to the mechanical aids used in manipulating the data. People sometimes say to me, "your machine does your thinking for you," and one colleague even alluded to "your history machine," apparently having in mind an assembly operation in which the rôle of the scholar was reduced to turning the switch to start the engines.

This is a little wide of the mark. First, the machine, or machines, for there are several, and the punch-cards are not an essential part of the project. The computations which they perform could be done without them, though at the cost of a far greater expenditure of labor. The punch-cards are nothing more than a filing-system, a means of disposing certain evidence so that it can be got at quickly when needed, and the machines are simply a means of counting the information in these files. Together these devices relieve the researcher of routine tasks, carry through computations more quickly and accurately than would otherwise be possible, and thus make feasible a larger number of computations in a given time. They affect the quantity and accuracy of the results, but not their character. Their work is not for that reason unimportant: they perform a humble but useful service.

The machines do not of course "think". On the contrary, the results they produce, the statistical tables, are in themselves no answer to any problem. The tables are merely arrangements of the evidence designed to test certain hypotheses. These arrangements must be planned before they are made and interpreted afterwards. They may or may not be significant, depending on what arguments are brought to bear. In other words, the problems of reasoning from statistics are not mechanical nor even mathematical; they are intellectual and historical. What remains to be done after the statistics are compiled is the theoretical work, the analysis. The validity of the conclusions of a statistical project depends, since a chain is as strong as its weakest link, on the correctness of the assumptions and definitions that precede the compilation of the figures and on the tightness of the logic in the inferences that are drawn from the final results.

The second general problem is the availability of the evidence. It is useless to attempt a statistical survey unless uniform and comparable information can be obtained for all or most of the men in the population being studied. This is not an easy matter, for historians must in general work from data that are fragmentary and scattered. The method is applicable, then, only to groups prominent enough and recent enough so that at least some documentation can be obtained for all or almost all of their members.

Even for the politicians of the 1840s information is not always easy to get. One might expect it to be otherwise. These men are relatively close to us in time as the subject-matter of history goes. Twelve of them even lived on into the twentieth century, the last, Francis Wemyss Charteris, tenth earl of Wemyss, dying in 1914 at the age of 96. Furthermore, secondary sources from which one can collect biographical information are already plentiful for the 1840s, though less abundant than they are for the decades immediately following. Besides the standard works available for the history of parliament in earlier periods as well, the student working in the post-1832 era can also draw on the successive editions of Dod's *Parliamentary Companion*, a wealth of contemporary genealogical works of all kinds, biographies and memoirs in profusion, local histories, local directories, obituaries in the *Annual Register* and the *Gentleman's Magazine*, contemporary lists of railway directors and of other types of businessmen, the invaluable *Post Magazine, Almanack, and Court and Parliamentary Register*, prospectuses and printed half-yearly reports of business concerns, business advertisements in the contemporary press, the splendid collection of manuscript minutes of meetings of railway directors assembled in the recently created Transport Commission Archives, and still other classes of materials which it would take too long to recapitulate. Collections of private papers for the nineteenth century are already very considerable; I have, however, found them less valuable for this kind of work than secondary sources. Though they are full of other useful information they yield relatively little in proportion to the labor expended on social background, economic and professional interests, and other biographical facts. More important, they give detailed information only for a few individuals, not for the entire group.

Yet even for this recent and highly documented period the difficulties of assembling precise information on a large number of subjects about a large number of men are formidable to a degree that would scarcely be credited by anyone who has not attempted this kind of research. The sources are, to varying degrees, inaccurate, carelessly compiled, and contradictory, and yield evidence that cannot be compared, since they deal with different things or describe situations existing at different times. Such problems, though the usual lot of the researcher, are multiplied when one must solve them for many individuals and also, if possible, bring the information into comparable form.

Small tasks that appear easy have proved unexpectedly troublesome as, for example, ascertaining the exact number who sat in this parliament, their names, and their dates of birth and death. The blue book of 1878, though invaluable, is not always accurate, other sources differ wildly on names and dates, and some rather intricate comparisons had to be made. The information, as might be expected, is uneven. While we know something, though by no means everything, about such familiar figures as Palmerston or Bright, other men, such as Daniel Henry Farrell, who was seated for Athlone on a petition in 1842 and unseated on a counterpetition in 1843, are so obscure that they seem to have disappeared almost beyond recall.

Mystifying questions of identity provide traps for the unwary. Among the men who sat in this parliament, Sir Rowland Hill (who became 2nd Viscount Hill in 1842) was a very different person from the man of penny postage fame; Henry Home Drummond was not the banker and Irvingite who founded the chair of political economy at Oxford; John Campbell Colquhoun was not the writer on psychical research who bore the identical three names; and W. E. Gladstone is to be distinguished from his contemporary William Gladstone, the eminent businessman. These points can gradually be teased out of the evidence, but they remain to plague the student, for the problem of identity must be solved afresh every time a possible reference to one of these men crops up in any of the sources.

Even relatively reliable sources contain errors on matters about which one would assume there could be no dispute. John Bell, M.P. for Thirsk, died in 1857 according to the 1871 edition of Burke's *Landed Gentry*, though other sources give his death date as 1851. Possibly Burke confused him with the notorious smuggler also named John Bell who did die in 1857 at the age of 110. Henry Broadwood, M.P. for Bridgwater, is wrongly recorded in the blue book of 1878 as having sat for Frome in the parliament of 1847–52, apparently because of a confusion with the man who follows next on the same page. The *Dictionary of National Biography* gives the birth date of Joshua Scholefield, M.P. for

Birmingham, as 1744 instead of the correct date, 1775. The *Gentleman's Magazine* and the *Annual Register* describe Peter Greenall, the member for Wigan who died in 1845, as a banker. This statement is unconfirmed and is almost certainly incorrect; apparently the M.P. was confused with his brother John Greenall who was for twenty-six years a partner in Parr, Lyon & Greenall.[17] These are only a few examples out of hundreds that could be cited.

On these matters the facts have been established. Unfortunately there are other points on which no sure information can be obtained. Often we know that a man had a given business interest but cannot be certain that he had it at the time that this parliament was in session. Many facts may be suspected which cannot be proved. The evidence gives tantalizing hints which there is no means of confirming, and I have reason to believe that a considerable number of business interests of M.P.'s have been excluded from these tabulations by the rather strict standards of evidence that I have adopted. Terminology in the nineteenth century is loose; though the word "merchant" generally bears the meaning given it in the *Oxford English Dictionary*, it is occasionally stretched to include an ironmaster like Edmund Buckley or a merchant banker like Thomas Baring. Sources disagree on essential facts and delicate problems of historical criticism occur, many of which cannot be solved on the basis of the information that has come down to us. Though each point is a small matter by itself, it is on the sum total of such points that the larger structure is reared, and the details must be rigorously handled if the conclusions are to be sound. The task is not impossible. The documentation, though not satisfactory nor complete, is sufficient for a fairly extended and unquestionably significant tabulation of biographical information. Yet the gaps and the conflicts in the information are distressing. Ultimately the worker on this type of project must resign himself to the fact that his results, no matter how massive, will never be complete and will contain an irreducible minimum of error.

There are other classes of facts that one cannot even attempt to tabulate. The scope of a project of this kind is limited by practical considerations such as the immense labor of compiling information even on a few points, or such as the danger, if too many variables are included, of producing results so complex that they are unintelligible. The point of unintelligibility is reached sooner than one might expect.

Hence it is necessary to adopt rigid rules of exclusion and abide by them, which means leaving out a good many interesting facts which, though they may be referred to in the text, cannot be covered by the tables.

Other information must be omitted because it is unavailable or because it cannot be obtained for enough men in the population to make a significant sample. It would have been desirable to include religious persuasion as a variable, but, to my surprise, no certain means could be found of identifying the Dissenters, though I have reason to believe they were few in number, while to separate Anglicans into High Church and Low Church would have been out of the question. Information on investments, of an amount that would be worth tabulating, was impossible to get; this would perhaps be the case for a contemporary parliament. I had hoped at one time to discover the holdings of these men in the funds, and have this information for a few, but the labor involved in handling the records proved an insurmountable obstacle to getting it for all. There are more intangible things which cannot possibly be treated statistically: individual influences, feelings, and emotional commitments, beliefs and opinions, views about what the facts were and what goals were desirable, likes and dislikes, habits of mind, and irrational fears and prejudices. These matters may be highly important, but our information on them is uncertain, and we could never hope to get such information for more than a small fraction of the entire group.

The most difficult of the three general problems proved to be the third, the classification of the evidence. The reason for the difficulty is simply this. Statistics is a technique for summarizing similar facts. Unfortunately, however, historical facts are not exactly similar; each is unique. We use the method to count characteristics that men have in common, but men have these characteristics in common only in a loose manner of speaking. We count, for example, the number of men in a given parliament or, within that group, the sons of peers, the railway directors, or the merchants. Yet in each of these cases it could be argued that the category selected does not tell the whole story and is not even fine enough to reflect the important qualifications in the evidence. The son of a baron whose title has been created the year before and the son of a duke whose title goes back many generations are not "peers' sons" in quite the same sense. The category of "railway directors" will include such major railway figures as George Hudson and Edmund Beckett Denison, but it will also include men whose concern with railways was merely incidental, landed magnates who accepted positions on the boards of small railways running in the vicinity of their estates. The term "merchant," even in its stricter sense, covered several different kinds of activities; it could be applied to a great international trader or to a manufacturer who maintained a wholesale warehouse to dispose of his product. One could even argue that not all these men were in the same sense members of parliament. Lord Ernest Augustus Charles Brudenell Bruce, who represented Marlborough for forty-six years, and Christopher Rice Mansel Talbot, who sat for fifty-five years for Glamorganshire, are both reported never to have spoken on the floor of the house of commons.[18] Did a seat in the house have the same meaning for them that it did for Shaftesbury or Cobden? And, if it did not, is it right to lump all four of these men together in a single category as "members of parliament"?

The degree of variation in each of these instances could be cut down by devising smaller and more refined classes, and in some cases this is the thing that must be done. Yet the categories cannot be made watertight except by refining them far beyond what is practicable, indeed in the last resort only by setting up a separate category for each characteristic of each individual, which would make nonsense of the work. To obtain classifications that can be used one must stop a good deal short of perfection. Very detailed categories are difficult to handle and produce results so complicated as to be unintelligible and so small that they prove nothing. Any usable set of categories is a compromise which will not reflect the evidence completely and which will probably contain variations and incongruities that the scholar who has worked closely with his materials will be disinclined to accept. Statistics is not an exact method, and a statistical presentation will contain only an approximation of the truth.

From this point several things follow. The scholar must be guided by his knowledge of what is left out of the tabulations as well as what is included in them, and must take care not to draw inferences which, though consistent with the figures which he cites, do violence to the evidence which he has had to omit. He must also play fair with the reader by explaining the criteria for each category and calling attention to the possible sources of distortion. A statistical presentation in which the basis of classification is not explained is worthless. Above all, in designing his categories, he must steer as best as he can between the two extremes of too little detail and too much, between categories so broad that they contain too great an amount of variation and seriously misrepresent the evidence and categories so fine that they are useless. There are no rules for doing this. It cannot be too strongly emphasized that the basis of classification is not the mechanical application of a formula, but the judgment of the scholar about the character of the materials and the purposes for which they may fairly be used.

Classification is the more difficult because the categories must generally be settled in advance before the bulk of the research is done. A preliminary enunciation of the questions is an essential condition for the collection of uniform answers. Yet in work of any complexity not all contingencies can be foreseen: cases will occur that do not fit the original classifications, and evidence that at the outset did not seem worth including may acquire significance in the later stages of the investigation and must in some fashion be brought in. It is difficult to prevent the handling of the categories from becoming a kind of scramble, with major changes being introduced long after the proper time. Pilot studies, small preliminary forays into the evidence, offer a partial but not altogether adequate escape from this dilemma.

It might be useful to show by a few illustrations how these difficulties occur. Probably the most aggravating problem has been handling social connections. In the first place there exists no usable vocabulary for this kind of material. The social history of the nineteenth century has been told in such terms as "aristocrat," "gentry," and "middle class," expressions which are too vague to serve as a framework for handling the detailed data. While some men can be unhesitatingly described as "aristocrats" or "businessmen," there are uncomfortably many borderline cases to which it is difficult to give a fixed designation, and it is obviously impossible to describe a group when one cannot be sure just who belonged to it. I have preferred, therefore, to disregard such general terms, and instead to tabulate only such facts as could be precisely determined. While one cannot speak exactly of aristocrats or businessmen, one can speak exactly of sons of peers, men who were listed in the edition of Burke's *Landed Gentry* contemporary to this parliament, manufacturers, or shipowners.

Objective classifications of this kind cannot, of course, be equated with the traditional catch phrases. It would be incorrect to say that the landed gentry of the 1840's consisted solely of men listed in the contemporary edition of Burke, partly because this early edition did not include men who might well have been described as landed gentry by their contemporaries, but partly also because the term "landed gentry" has no fixed meaning and cannot, therefore, be properly equated with anything. The point is rather that it is more satisfactory to work with an unambiguous definition, even if reservations must be stated about it in the text and allowance made for possible distortion, than to work with a definition that is subjective and uncertain.

The intricacy of the social connections of the members of this parliament caused a difficulty of a different kind. Many of these men were related to the peerage, baronetage, or landed gentry in several ways and could be classified under more than one heading. I had originally hoped to include in the final figures as complete an account as could be given of these various connections. On this point, however, I have been forced to retreat, for the earliest tabulations produced patterns too complex to be handled or understood. Ultimately it proved necessary to exclude refinements that I had originally put in, and to set up a new series of mutually exclusive categories in which each man was listed only once by what appeared to be his closest or most significant social connection. Even this system has not been altogether easy to apply. In some instances it was hard to decide which of two alternatives was the social connection by which a man should be listed. Yet the troublesome cases have been relatively few in number, and on the whole the device of assigning only one social classification to each man has worked fairly well. On some other points mutually exclusive categories proved impracticable. It would have been advantageous to use them for economic interests, but there were too many men with more than one significant business interest, and here fullness of detail seemed more important than convenience in manipulation. In a smaller but parallel matter, mutually exclusive categories could not be set up for the universities these men attended, since several M.P.'s attended more than one.

Some classes of data were too complicated to classify at all and had to be excluded. I found no means, for example, of handling systematically the influences and pressures upon these men in their constituencies. The incidence of patronage was too varied to permit tabulation, while pressures from the electorate and, indirectly, from the un-enfranchised would have been still harder to catch. More general points about a constituency, its location, whether it was a county or a borough, the number of registered electors, and whether the member had a residence in it, were of course easy to classify and have been included in the tabulations.

Another troublesome problem was settling a date after which no evidence would be admitted. A historical situation is difficult to describe statistically because it is constantly changing. Men marry, inherit estates and titles, or acquire new business interests, and it is desirable to include as much of this information as possible in the figures. One way to meet the difficulty of dating is to describe, as Sir Lewis Namier did, a situation existing at a particular moment. Yet even this procedure can, as he has shown, produce anomalies, and in any case I preferred for several reasons to study an entire parliament over a six-year period. A watertight system of handling these changes would have been too complicated to use. The problem admitted of no entirely satisfactory solution. To take 1841 as the basic date would have ex-cluded important business interests acquired during the course of this parliament, while using 1847 would have introduced even more disturbing anomalies: it would have meant, among other things, de-scribing in terms of their 1847 circumstances men who by that time were in the house of lords, were dead, or for other good reasons were no longer in the house of commons. Rather complicated rules had finally to be adopted, and even so a certain amount of latitude had to be allowed.

A final illustration might be given, of quite a different character, the handling of votes. The problem here was not, as it was in most other cases, due to incomparable, inaccurate or incomplete data. On the contrary, information on votes is highly comparable, more reliable (despite occasional lapses) than any other large class of facts, and overwhelming in its abundance. The problem was to reduce this bulk of material to manageable proportions. This might have been done by including only one division on each issue, but this would have meant losing the opinions of men who did not vote in that particular division but did vote in similar ones. It finally proved possible to summarize information on votes by using cumulative scales of the Guttman type which, for the members of this parliament, have worked out un-expectedly well.

Even after all these problems have been dealt with, the results of a statistical study must be regarded with caution and suspicion. Statistical tables produce a false sense of security. The complicated analysis and summary of the data gives the final exposition a misleading appearance of precision. As a counterweight to this it should always be remembered that the method is not exact. "It is an easy and fatal step to think that the accuracy of our arithmetic is equivalent to the accuracy of our knowledge about the problem in hand."[19] Even if manual errors are kept to a minimum—and they are an almost inescapable hazard in a project of any size—the accuracy of the results still depends upon the accuracy of the data assembled and these, as I have been at some pains to show, are subject in many ways to error.

Statistics are, further, a dangerous weapon and can, in the hands of the unskilled or the unscrupulous, be used to misrepresent the facts in many ways. Incorrectly used, they can be as misleading in their fashion as general impressions can in theirs. It is tempting and easy and fatally mistaken to make the conclusions go further than the evidence can carry. To give what is perhaps the best-known example of such a pitfall, a statistical correlation does not prove the existence of a cause and effect relationship. Such a correlation may be accidental, it may be due to some third element, possibly one not included in the tabulations at all, or it may be due to some feature of the figures that does not at first strike the eye. In a complex situation causation is likely to be multiple, and for any one set of figures several plausible explanations are often possible. An excellent example of this *pons asinorum* is the finding which emerged from my study of the parliament of 1841 that men related to the peerage or gentry were more likely to be bachelors than were those less well connected. A colleague to whom I described this discovery suggested an intriguing explanation for it which had to do with the difficulty of obtaining suitable parties to a marriage in families of exalted rank. However, a simpler hypothesis can also be suggested. Two other findings were that social position is statistically related to age and that age is statistically related, as one might expect, to marital status. In other words, men with social position tended to enter parliament when younger, and the young men in this parliament were on the whole more likely to be bachelors than their seniors. Most of these well-born bachelors had in fact married by the time they reached the age of thirty.

A limitation on the method of a different kind, and one not always remembered, is that it is principally useful not for originating hypotheses but for testing hypotheses that have already been formulated. This lends the method something of a negative cast: one is unlikely to arrive at final explanations by statistics alone and the use of statistics without theory will probably not rise above a rather crude level of empiricism. One cannot simply stir all the facts together and see what emerges, attractive as the proposal sounds. The number of possible correlations is too large. Since it is impracticable to follow up all lines, statistics must to a large extent be guided, and limited accordingly, by a deliberate selection of evidence based on theory.

I have dealt very fully with the practical difficulties of the application of quantitative techniques to history. In conclusion I would like to say that these difficulties do not invalidate the method, in comparison with other alternatives. It would be an unfortunate error to assume that more precise generalizations can be made without statistics than with them, or that when statistics cannot produce a correct answer a general impression can. On the contrary, these difficulties are not the exclusive property of the statistical method. They occur, though they may not always be noticed or remembered, in any conscientious attempt to make general statements about large questions of historical interpretation. They are inherent in problems of historical generalization, and are due to the incompleteness, variety, and complexity of the materials with which the historian must work.

Indeed it is a merit of the method that, by enforcing an orderly arrangement of the evidence, it calls attention to limitations in our information or possible flaws in our reasoning that we might otherwise forget or fail to observe. In this sense the "disadvantages" of a quantitative method, the problems which the researcher must face, are actually advantages, for they help to chart the limits of our knowledge. We know, from the way in which we have devised the definitions, what we are omitting, and we know, from the figures given in the results, exactly how far our generalizations must be qualified.

It is a mistake to suppose that a quantitative approach distorts history into extremes of black and white, or that it necessitates the use of absolute and sweeping statements. Its effect is exactly the opposite: it compels the user to avoid absolute pronouncements and to appreciate the limitations and exceptions to every generalization that is put forward. One might refer here to Professor Kendall's statement, in his inaugural lecture, that "perhaps the most characteristic feature of the statistical method" is that "it recognizes frankly that outside the domain of pure mathematics, deductive logic itself, and similar subjects which are concerned with logical relations between ideas or the syntactic construction of language, few, if any, meaningful statements are certain."[20] Perhpas a method which recognizes uncertainty and takes it as a starting point is particularly suited to handle the complex data of history. It is a sensitive instrument of analysis in that it enables us to state with clarity and precision the ambiguities, inconsistencies, and incompleteness of the material.

NOTES

1. "The House of Commons in the 1840s," *History* (new series), **XXXIX**, 137 (October 1954), pp. 249—262.

2. Charles A. Beard, *An economic interpretation of the constitution of the United States* (1913).

3. Sir Lewis Namier, *The structure of politics at the accession of George III*, 2 vols. (1929); *England in the age of the American revolution* (1930). J. E. Neale, *The Elizabethan House of Commons* (1949); *Elizabeth I and her parliaments, 1559—1581* (1953). D. Brunton and D. H. Pennington, *Members of the Long Parliament* (1954).

4. Crane Brinton, *The Jacobins* (1930).

5. Donald M. Greer, *The incidence of the terror during the French revolution* (1935); *The incidence of emigration during the French revolution* (1951).

6. William Miller, 'American historians and the business élite', *Journal of economic history*, **IX**, 2 (November 1949); 'The recruitment of the business élite', *Quarterly journal of economics*, **LXIV**, 2 (May 1950); 'American lawyers in business and politics', *Yale law journal*, **LX**, 1 (January 1951); 'The business elite in business bureaucracies', *Men in business: essays in the history of entrepreneurship* (1952).

7. C. Wright Mills, 'The American business elite: a collective portrait', *Journal of economic history*, Supp. V (December 1945).

8. H. Dewey Anderson, 'The educational and occupational attainments of our national rulers', *Scientific monthly*, **40** (June 1935). Harold J. Laski, 'The personnel of the British cabinet, 1801—1924', *Studies in law and politics* (1932).

9. Dale A. Hartman, 'British and American ambassadors: 1893–1930', *Economica*, **XI** (August 1931). Robert T. Nightingale, 'The personnel of the British foreign office and diplomatic service', *American political science review*, **24** (May 1930).

10. Hans Gerth, 'The Nazi party: its leadership and composition', *American Journal of sociology*, **45** (January 1940).

11. For a more extended discussion of this literature see Richard Hofstadter, 'Beard and the constitution: the history of an idea', *American quarterly*, **II**, 3 (Fall 1950).

12. Bernard Cracroft, 'The analysis of the house of commons, or indirect representation', *Essays on reform* (1867).

13. Edmund Burke, 'Reflections on the revolution in France . . .' *Works* (1815 ed.), pp. 89–92.

14. Paul Leicester Ford, ed., *The writings of Thomas Jefferson . . .* **i** (1892), p. 82.

15. Boswell's *Life of Johnson*, Friday, 18 April 1783.

16. Hofstadter, *Op. cit.*, p. 204.

17. Theodor E. Gregory, *The Westminster Bank through a century* (1936), **ii**, p. 25. I am indebted to Dr. T. C. Barker of the London School of Economics for pointing out this discrepancy.

18. Earl of Cardigan, *The Wardens of Savernake Forest* (1949), p. 308. Frederic Boase, *Modern biography . . .* (1892–1921), **iii**, p. 869.

19. M. J. Moroney, *Facts from figures* (1951), p. 3. I am also greatly indebted, for the more general parts of this discussion, to L. H. C. Tippett, *Statistics* (1943).

20. M. G. Kendall, 'The statistical approach', *Economica*, new series, **XVII** (May 1950), p. 139.

CHAPTER 6

CORRESPONDENCE WITH PROFESSOR J.H. HEXTER

(The first of these letters, mine to Mr. Hexter of 29 March, 1967, was a response to his request for my comments on a long paper of his which at that time bore the title "Historiography." This paper was written for and has now been published by the *International Encyclopedia of the Social Sciences* (**6**, New York, 1968, pp. 368—394), with the title "The Rhetoric of History" under the general heading "HISTORIOGRAPHY." Readers who wish a more extended statement of Mr. Hexter's views should examine this article, which was really the opening gun in the correspondence. Mr. Hexter will give further attention to these and related matters in the book he refers to at the end of his letter of 4 April 1967, which will be entitled *The History Primer* and will be published by Basic Books late in 1970. The remaining correspondence developed out of this original interchange. The last three letters, written in 1970, deal with some additional points that Mr. Hexter wanted to clarify and on which I also had something to say. The letters are published as they were originally written except for minor corrections.)

1 AYDELOTTE TO HEXTER, 29 MARCH 1967

Department of History
University of Iowa
Iowa City, Iowa

Dear Jack:

I was stimulated and excited by your essay, "Historiography," as I have not been by anything for a long while. It is marvellously well written, and I admire the stylistic elegance, the tightness of argument, and the sharpness of focus. I have spent time on it because I wanted to clarify my own ideas on these problems. I accept a great deal of what you say but I do have some reservations and, since you ask for criticism, I will try to summarize a few of them. These points, however, though I regard some of them as fairly serious, do not change the fact that my reaction to your essay as a whole was decidedly positive.

1. One possible objection to your argument is that, in your attempt to differentiate history from science, you employ stereotyped conceptions of each area of inquiry and that, if you took account of the full diversity of behavior in each field, the degree of overlapping might be even greater than you allow. I have always found history difficult to define, in view of the great variety of *good* practice. Science may be even harder to delimit, and some of the most eminent scientists have denied that there is any such thing as "the scientific method." I have quoted these views to you before, and your reaction was that, if one takes so extreme a position, it is impossible to make intelligible distinctions. Nevertheless, this is the position that several Nobel prizewinners do take and, if they do, I should suppose that their opinions as to the nature of the work in which they have achieved pre-eminence ought to be listened to with respect. You may recall that Abraham Kaplan in *The Conduct of Inquiry* (p. 27) deliberately refrains from defining "scientific method" because he believes that "there is no one thing to be defined" and that one could as well speak of "the method" for baseball. He uses as an analogy for science the game you use as an analogy for history.

I wonder, for example, if you do not push your case too hard when you suggest that in science there should be no gap between cognition and written communication; certainly such a gap existed for Darwin for many years. On the other hand, your proposition that historians may know much about the past which they cannot communicate in writing, though I would in part assent to it, may be incomplete or one-sided. It is a common experience that writing stimulates thinking and that a person often doesn't fight his way through, or even come to grips with, or perhaps even identify, the most significant and the toughest problems until he reaches the writing stage. Is it not possible that, on this point, you exaggerate the proclivities of both scientists and historians: that the separation of knowledge from the communication of it may not be so small for the first or so large for the second as you represent it?

It could also be argued that scientific investigation is often less logical and more subjective than you allow. You say that most historians would be at a loss to explain their particular choices of hypotheses or of records to investigate. Yet something of this is often alleged to be true for scientific inquiry as well. Scientists hit upon hypotheses in odd, fantastic, and often inexplicable ways, and it is by no means always clear what materials it will be most fruitful to use to test them. The problem of the relative expediencies of alternative taxonomies occurs for scientists too, since they can get different kinds of results with different arrangements of the evidence and, for them as well as for historians, it can be a matter of debate which features of the evidence it is most useful to bring out. I have the feeling that you attribute to science a degree of finality and precision that most scientists would not now claim. The story one hears more often is that scientific theories can never be proved, only disproved; and, further, that the absence of disproof is seldom conclusive since the points of contact between a major scientific theory and the available evidence may be limited: parts of the theory can be tested, while other parts are merely conjectural extrapolation. Some of your arguments about science appear to have a bit of a nineteenth-century flavor, and to rest upon an old view of science that would today be highly qualified.

2. I am not sure that you do full justice to the analytical philosophers. I don't dispute part of your thesis about them. Indeed, your treatment of the dilemma they face, in trying to deal with historical scholarship, is admirable, one of the best things in the essay. Your use of the analogy of epicycles, quadrants, and equants is brilliant. All that you say here needs to be said, and your statement constitutes a clear advance in the argument. I trust I am correct in understanding that you do not seek to refute Hempel *in toto*, but that you merely insist that what he says applies to only part of the work that historians do and cannot be accepted as a complete or exclusive definition of their activities. I note that you concede the similarity of some of the objectives of historical writing and of scientific writing. Granting all that you say, however, I still feel that the analytical philosophers have made a substantial contribution, and that they are not so ridiculous as you make them appear. It was a merit of your paper that you did not claim, as many have done and as some still do, that the logical processes of history are

essentially different from the logical processes of the natural sciences. Hence, we didn't have to waste time on that silly argument. The service the analytical philosophers have rendered is that they have protested against this nonsense and have insisted that logic was unitary, the same wherever applied, a point that seems indeed obvious enough, but well worth making considering how much deference had been paid to the contrary position. I also think that Hempel, within the sphere we would both allow to him, has some sensible things to say.

3. Coming now to more general matters, I believe the difference between us, so far as I can identify it, may lie in our appraisals of the present condition and present needs of the historical profession. I doubt that we are far apart on fundamentals. I concede that historians do engage in narrative and description, that they are not exclusively (and in some cases very little) concerned with general laws, and that they may build up an understanding of the past that is not reducible to general laws. You concede that it is all right for historians to try to formulate and verify general statements once in a while, and we would agree that the choice of procedures depends on what is appropriate for a particular problem or a particular investigation. Yet I think there is, between us, a difference of emphasis. You are concerned to assert the liberty of historians from an exclusive commitment to the covering-law model. I, on the other hand, am worried about what I consider to be wide-spread deficiencies in modern historical practice. I believe that it could admit of some improvement, and the line of improvement I have in mind is one that would perhaps assimilate it more closely to the popular notion of scientific method. I wish that historians in general were more thoughtful, careful and responsible in regard to (a) analysis and theory and (b) the verification of general statements. I don't concede that the present practice of the history profession is everything that could be desired on these points. You say that, for the standards of historiography, it is possible to follow the consensus of "the better historians." Yet some of the deficiencies I object to appear in the writings of even the most eminent practitioners. I regard Namier as the most distinguished English historian of his generation, but even he occasionally makes wild statements that bear no discernible relation to his evidence and that do not appear to have been rigorously thought through. Such intellectual carelessness on the part of so great a man

may be due, I fear, not to individual recalcitrance toward accepted professional standards, but to the absence of adequate professional standards in regard to theory and the verification of general statements. Historians have in general, I feel, not given proper attention to these two matters. We seem to view the present state of affairs differently. You find a number of benighted historians who labor under the illusion that they are or ought to be scientists. For me, the profession appears heavily populated by individuals who regard it as an insult to be asked to substantiate the simplest general statement. Perhaps we both exaggerate the number of those with whom we disagree.

4. I want to extend my remarks about the importance of theory. I agree with you that the derivation of general laws or, what is more feasible, generalizations on a limited scale need not be the sole business of historians, but I would put the emphasis in a different place. You would like to tell historians that they are free not to do this, whereas I would like to tell them that they are free to do it and ought to do more of it, and more carefully. I don't think that historians on the whole have given enough thought to the opportunities for building up general statements. There may, however, be more of this kind of thing now than there used to be and, if this is true, I would regard this increased theoretical concern as one of the great and useful innovations in modern historical study. I agree with you that dull history is bad history to the extent that it is dull, but I do not assent to the proposition, which some readers might think you imply, that dullness can be avoided simply by evocative writing. Dullness is a tricky subject, for what is exciting to some people may be dull to others, and this is not just a matter of differences in level of sophistication but also of differences in interest and concern. My general point here is that dullness can be an intellectual as well as an emotional problem, and that vivid writing and emotional transference are not necessarily the sole means of eliminating it. A better means, in some cases, may be analysis and a direction of the argument toward large theoretical problems to which the subject-matter can be related. Some writers of popular history presumably communicate to their readers a lot of vicarious emotion but they are not, for me, interesting historians.

Nor is a narrative necessarily the best means to combat dullness. I cannot agree that the subject-matter of history is always interesting for its own sake. This certainly would not be true for my own research. The issues of British politics of a century and a quarter ago are now dead, and I can muster little enthusiasm for them. On the other hand, the votes and debates on these questions can be used to shed light on certain theoretical problems, the nature of political attitudes and why men hold them, that are still fresh and that interest me greatly. I have heard many papers that attempted to avoid dullness by telling a story or narrative, based on sound research, but uninformed by analytic interest. I react negatively to presentations like this and remain unmoved by what you refer to as the "confrontation with the riches of the event itself." I have just sat through two papers at our spring history conference that illustrate my point. One dealt with a small New England town for a few years in the mid-eighteenth century, a limited topic apparently, but the speaker used his detailed information to raise and discuss certain large questions about the social and economic aspects of the Great Awakening in a most useful and interesting way. The other paper dealt with a major episode in the history of the British Empire in the later eighteenth century, a large topic. It was based on careful research and obviously great knowledge, it told a highly dramatic story, but it made no effort to deal with the more general implications of the evidence, and I found it insufferably boring. Your insistence on the primary interest of the subject-matter recalls to my mind the publisher who advised Darwin to center his book (*The Origin of Species*) around pigeons, "because everybody is interested in pigeons."

5. I hold also that historians should try to verify their general statements, and that they have on the whole given insufficient consideration to the need and to the opportunities for doing this. I make no wild claims about the achievability of finality. On the contrary, my recent interest in problems of verification has sharpened my realization that a large element of what historians want to say and should say must inevitably be tentative and speculative. Nevertheless, I should like to see them do the best they can and my impression is that, though reasonably high standards prevail for verifying details, the general statements that historians make are often rather free-wheeling. I object when a historian, who has checked his detailed data carefully and makes scrupulously limited claims about it, goes on to talk like God

and the prophets when he comes to topics on which he has no substantive information whatever. Some historians, instead of presenting an increment to knowledge, simply gas about the subject in an inconclusive fashion, toss in a few cheesy epigrams and a little vivid writing, and let it go at that. The *TLS* is full of reviews that carry on in this way, and such activities are not restricted to the *TLS*. It is hard to control a writer who does this since he may cover himself by a qualifying adverb that absolves him of responsibility for what he says or, worse still, may put forth his ideas in so unclear a fashion as to deprive them of meaning and, as I said in one of my articles, a statement that has no clear meaning cannot be disproved.

6. What bothers me about the direction and emphasis of your paper is that I fear that your line of argument may be subject to abuse. I know that you would agree with my plea for a higher standard of professional responsibility in the development of theory and in the verification of general statements. You say nothing contrary to the proposition that the methods of historical thinking and communication should be as rigorous as the circumstances permit. Indeed you insist that the procedures you advocate would not open the way to intellectual slatternliness. Yet the line you take is one by which slatternly work is occasionally defended, and it can all too readily be used as a justification for slipshod historical writing of the sort that you would protest against as vigorously as anyone. While I concede the value of evocative language, it goes a little hard with me when you insist so frequently, in five different passages altogether, that one should sometimes sacrifice generality, precision, control, and exactness to evocative force and scope. This is done all the time, and the results are not invariably the kind of historical writing that you would applaud. I presume that Trevelyan was intending to sacrifice precision to evocative force when he said, in a lecture I heard him give, that the English rebelled against the House of Stuart in 1688 "because they were men." A similar intent doubtless lies behind the proposition that in the time of the Renaissance "the Heavens were rolled up as a scroll," a statement that does not particularly send me and that I do not believe adds greatly to our understanding of the period. Some modern writers to whom you would perhaps object certainly succeed in sacrificing precision to evocation and they would, I imagine, welcome your article

and regard it as giving support and justification for the kind of history they like to write. Doubtless you would repudiate such excesses. Yet I am not sure that the best way to combat them is to make the kind of recommendation that you make in the five passages of your typescript I have referred to. My own impression is that, at the moment, historians don't need to be exhorted to be more evocative, that they are already somewhat too evocative for their own good, and that they need to simmer down a little and look more carefully at what they are getting and what they are delivering.

Yours,
Bill

2 HEXTER TO AYDELOTTE, 4 APRIL 1967

Center for Advanced Study
in the Behavioral Sciences
Stanford, California

Dear Bill:

Thank you for your long and thoughtful letter dealing with my article on historiography. The careful and well-thought-out critique was even more satisfactory evidence of your interest in it than the generous fanfare of compliments with which you started.

I do think that it is, on the whole, as you say. Our area of substantial disagreement is relatively narrow while our appraisal of what needs to be emphasized within our area of agreement diverges considerably, although not, perhaps, as considerably as you think. I suspect that your impression as to that divergence is, at least in part, a consequence of my definition of my job in writing the article. Perhaps, I can substantiate this by referring you to a piece of mine published in the January 1967 issue of the *Journal of Contemporary History* where I indulge in some pretty pompous pontifications about history-writing in the past 25 years. I think that what I say there is substantially closer to your view than what I say in the article I sent you. This is due to the fact that I define my task in the historiography article as the problems involved in the process of writing history.

I am aware of the validity of the point you made about the overlap between the act of historical discovery and the act of communicating that discovery. Being a thoroughly unsystematic person in my mental habits, I know that frequently I only find out what I know in the process of writing about it. The point is, however, that I feel it appropriate, for my purposes, to separate the activity of historical discovery from that of historical discourse, to focus primarily, if not wholly, on the latter subject, and to raise all my questions directly in the context of what appears on the printed page with only very indirect reference to methods of investigation and research. It seems to me that this focus is a proper one, given the subject I was dealing with, which is not history in general but specifically historiography, defined as the writing of history, the rhetoric of history, or the structure of historical discourse.

This also accounts for an apparent difference between us, which you emphasize and which I do not think exists. When you talk about the difference and similarity between history and science and emphasize the similarity, you are focusing your attention on the psychology or logic of discovery. When I emphasize the difference, I focus on the actual structure and character of the finished product. On that point, I think it is proper and important to emphasize and explain the irreducibility of much of the form of historical discourse to the form or rhetoric of scientific discourse and that it is necessary to indicate clearly the points at which historical rhetoric is radically unassimilable to the appropriate rhetoric of the sciences. I hope I have done this persuasively and I hope, also, that I have not denied the frequent similarities of the requirements of historical and scientific statement.

I have been making an effort out here to expand and clarify some of the notions that I dealt with in my article for the *Encyclopaedia* and I will further take advantage of your good nature by sending you, under separate cover, copies of two chapters that are fairly close to being final drafts for the book that I hope ultimately to write on the subject.

Thank you very much, again, for your careful, critical comments, which I value very highly indeed.

Yours sincerely,
Jack

3. AYDELOTTE TO HEXTER, 14 JUNE 1967

Department of History
University of Iowa
Iowa City, Iowa

Dear Jack:

I read with pleasure your chapters II and III and your article in *The Journal of Contemporary History*. I agree with much of what you say, all the more because I have already said it myself: that the record of the past is insufficient, and yet too large for any man to grasp, two points I discussed in my generalization article, though you develop them more fully; that it is important not just to find the data but also to realize its significance, which was a principal argument of my quantification article; and the dangers of GIGO (*JCH* article, p. 18), about which I have also had something to say.

Though your stuff is beautifully written (obviously the result of hard labor) and readable and intelligent, I still have reservations about your emphasis, something on the lines of the long letter I wrote you about your paper, "Historiography." In regard to the *JHC* article, which was on the whole a nice article, I am still bothered by the fact that your strictures and admonitions and cautions are mainly on one side. You are very severe about the dangers of borrowing new methods and new techniques, though you are generous in admitting their value when properly used. All that you say about those dangers is sound enough, and your points are well taken. They seem to me somewhat obvious, but perhaps these things need to be said. I wish, however, that you had been equally severe about the dangers in the other direction, of making general statements that are not supported or examined so far as the circumstances permit. The sins of historians along this line seem to me more considerable and more widespread than the sins of historians along the other.

In other words, as I indicated in my earlier letter, you are more ready than I am to assume that present historical practice is acceptable. You appear to suggest that all that is needed, to lay down good principles of method, is to observe the practice of the better historians and to generalize from that. I, as you know, hold that many historians, even some of the best ones, have shown a certain irresponsibility in dogmatizing on subjects where the evidence is insufficient to support their conclusions. I don't mean that historians should attempt to achieve finality, but merely that they should do the best they can, and also that they should play fair with the reader by distinguishing between statements they are fairly sure of and statements they are less sure of. I find the general practice and tradition of the profession wanting in these respects. You would perhaps in part agree with me, but somehow you don't seem to take it so seriously.

My view is that historians have, as a profession, unduly neglected both problems of verification and also problems of theoretical analysis. I don't want to repeat what I said in the other letter, but I might give one small additional example relating to the second of these points. I agree with you, of course, as to the absurdity of the notion that a historian should try to approach the record of the past with "an open mind," thus disregarding the constructive efforts of his predecessors. Nevertheless, I know of historians who are still trying to do exactly this. I am acquainted with an eminent historian who works on the party history of the mid-nineteenth century, my period. He refuses to read the books of Michels and Duverger because of the danger that these theoretical analyses of the role and nature of parties might prejudice him in his interpretation of the evidence. This made quite an impression on me.

Turning to another side of the argument, I cannot help suspecting that, in your discussion of the social scientist in Chapter III, you may be setting up a straw man, a figure designed for easy demolition. I would argue that the ablest social scientists I have known are less rigid, narrow, and pedantic than you make them out to be. Although social scientists have been concerned with establishing more rigorous intellectual methods, I cannot agree with you that this excludes the pursuit of legitimate historical objectives, or that the conception of knowledge in the social sciences necessarily eliminates a dimension from knowing as men actually experience it. In general, in the social sciences as elsewhere, you simply try to do the best you can, taking into account what are the most useful questions to answer, what are the difficulties of answering them, and what kinds of effort are most likely to repay the labor. I cannot see the great gulf that you distinguish between the social sciences and history. I would agree that some social scientists may have been more conscientious and some historians, perhaps, more imaginative, but these are individual differences, not intrinsic in the nature of the fields. I find invalid your attempts, at the end of your third chapter, to distinguish between the kinds of statements a historian would accept and those a social scientist would accept. I believe that a social scientist would accept the imaginative and speculative statements you offer as illustrations provided, of course, that you presented them as conjectures, the most plausible that can be reached in the present state of our knowledge, and convincing to you for the reasons you indicate. The social sciences are full of conjectures of this kind. Again, you say that a historian should make use of the experience of his own life in his intellectual work. Do you imagine that a social scientist doesn't? If so, you are much mistaken. The social sciences contain plenty of insights that are arrived at in something like this way. Similarly, your implication that we deal with our own problems in scholarly study applies, surely, to all forms of creative work. Nor, I would argue, is this necessarily unscientific.

I hope these few examples will be enough to indicate the general line of my reaction.

With all good wishes,
Bill

4. HEXTER TO AYDELOTTE, 19 JANUARY 1970

Department of History
Yale University
New Haven, Conn.

Dear Bill:

Thank you very much for your interest in publishing our previous correspondence and for the chance you offer me to add any subsequent thoughts I have had on the matter it deals with.

I am grateful for the opportunity to make some additions because of two things that have happened since our exchange of letters. First, in the interval I have given some time and attention—perhaps an inordinate and unprofitable amount of both—to issues about which we corresponded. Second, in Chicago in the summer of 1969, by the courtesy of the Committee on Mathematical and Statistical Methods in History, of the Mathematical Social Science Board, I was able to attend a meeting of historians active in the application of sophisticated mathematical and statistical techniques to historical data. These two activities have enabled me to sort out what has hitherto puzzled me somewhat in the encounters between you and me. What has happened in those encounters is that we found very little mutual disagreement on general principles; but that both of us ended our exchange of apparently identical news with the unallayed suspicion that our general agreements in principle papered over quite considerable disagreements in practice.

This does not greatly surprise me, but it does point to a significant trait of historians, one that I emphasized in my article on "The Rhetoric of History (sub. HISTORIOGRAPHY)" in the *International Encyclopedia of Social Sciences*, and one that I think requires further emphasis. It is that the programmatic statements of historians, their utterances about their intellectual commitments or philosophy of history or methodology (what a pretentious term!) or general intentions, are very bad indicators of their actual practice. What they say they intend to do, what they say historians ought to do or need to do, often are widely at variance with what they actually do. I think my friend Lawrence Stone provides an excellent instance of this sort of variance. In his programmatic statements, he is strongly committed to quantitative and statistical techniques, to "analytical history" and to the systematic application of the social sciences to historical investigation and discourse. In actual practice he does occasionally use these resources with very good effect, but he does not let himself be tied to or constricted by his philosophical or theoretical commitments, and occasionally he "uses" such techniques as nineteenth-century roués were said to use ladies of easy virtue, again often with good effect. I happen to think that this is all for the best, but best or worst, it is evidently so, as a careful examination of his fine book, *The Crisis of the Aristocracy, 1558–1641*, reveals. This is the point, or one of the points, of an extraordinarily long examination of the book that I perpetrated in *The Journal of British Studies*.

It seems to me that this observed deviation between principle and practice applies to you, and that its application was evident in your relation to the group of historians gathered in Chicago and in your estimate of their performance. At that gathering the deviation of your kind of historical commitment from mine became much more sharply evident than it ever has been in our conversations. That group of historians is to a considerable extent your brood. They are outstanding representatives in the last couple of generations of historians with a strong commitment to quantification. In your case that commitment goes back more than three decades. I find it rather harder to specify what my own commitment has been, since I do not think I have ever formulated it very systematically. I suppose it would come to a sort of gross loose-minded eclecticism with respect to method that will grab at whatever at the moment looks like the handiest tool for dealing with each historical problem as it emerges in my mind from a consideration of the record. Anyhow, when I look over the history that I have written, that seems to me as close as I can come to a reasonable characterization of what I have done.

I am sure that at the meeting in Chicago I must have conveyed to you some sense of my uneasiness not so much about what was being done there by your sequelae as about the way it was being done (assuming that one can wholly separate what is being done from the way it is done in history, a contrafactual assumption).

Two related things bothered me most. The first was a certain deafness on the part of the quantifying and mathematizing historians to what the outsiders and critics were saying. The second was the sense that too many of those historians were negligent of, and a few were simply contemptuous of, common language as the appropriate vocabulary and rhetoric for historical writing. I was not alone in feeling that the more critical participants at the meeting—Roberts, Hanham, and I—were courteously listened to but not effectively heard. Indeed I remember an outburst of Ted Rabb's in which he explicitly made this point. He said that our criticisms were at least laid on the same target, that they did represent a coherent challenge to some of the assumptions of most of the participants, and that no one in that group had seriously tried to understand them much less to counter them. I do not think that Rabb's perceptions in this matter were faulty.

What I would like to do here is reproduce my own remarks at the session as well as I can remember them. As I recall, the circumstances were that Lawrence Stone's paper, on which I was supposed to comment, had not yielded much in the way of positive results, so I felt free to address myself to more general problems. My taking-off point was some remarks made on the previous day by a political scientist at the meeting. He had said that among the social sciences psychology and economics were the most highly developed, political science and sociology the next most highly developed, and history the least developed. I will now try to reproduce my remarks.

In reading the papers distributed and listening to the comments on them, it would seem to me that in the pursuit of sophisticated quantitative and statistical methods, many of the historians present here have lost control over one of history's indispensable resources—the common language of ordinary spoken and written discourse. Consider Mr.————'s use of the word "developed." The assumption would ordinarily be that his language is value-free. Yet it is clear that for him the term "developed" is honorific, and that the more "developed" the discipline is, the better. But he has used the term "developed" without even indicating in what respect the disciplines he speaks of are developed. In context, however, it is clear that by "developed" he means mathematized or quantified, and that he is in fact committed to the view that the more highly mathematical and quantified a social science is, the better it is.

Yet there is no *a priori* reason for believing that this is so. Indeed, one might argue that at the other extreme from the pejorative "underdeveloped" is an equally pejorative "overdeveloped". Thus, for example, it is possible to say of a man that his muscles are overdeveloped. In that case, further development of his muscles is not advantageous but disadvantageous, since he is already, in common language, muscle-bound. I would suggest that history certainly, and the social sciences possibly, can be severely hampered in their quest for understanding by excessive development of their mathematizing and quantifying aspects to the neglect of the overall harmony of their growth.

To judge by the papers that I have read for this meeting, the element of historiography that is being obliterated by an overgrowth of quantification is aptitude for saying what one has in mind in clear, ordinary prose. What I note in some of these papers, as in the remarks of Mr.————, is a lack of mastery of their native tongue. It may be argued that the payoff in sophisticated quantification overbalances this loss of mastery. This is an argument which I reject. Carried to the extreme, it would mean that history, if sufficiently quantified, could do without common language altogether. This is not a mere hallucination on my part. In fact, the point was put to me by one of the mathematizing historians here present. I would like to regard it as a joke, but I am not at all sure that it was intended as a joke. It is a purpose which, if ever achieved, will be a horror.

It may also be argued that, in order to break new ground in the area of quantification, it is necessary, for the time being, to concentrate on mathematical and statistical techniques to the neglect of skill in ordinary prose exposition. I do not find this view acceptable either. It reminds me of an old cliché used by the communists back in the thirties to excuse some of the more painful aberrations of the Soviet fatherland. It went, "You can't make an omelet without breaking eggs." George Orwell's response to this cliché was, "Sooner or later somebody is going to ask 'But where is the omelet?'" After examining the papers for this session, that question seems most appropriate to me in the present context. Gentlemen, where is the omelet?

That, at least, is how I like to remember what I said. What I actually did say was probably a good bit ruder and less tidy. The point, however, remains. I do not for a moment suggest that historians who do not focus almost all their energies on quantification and mathematization necessarily produce gems of historical discourse; both of us know better than that. I do suggest most strongly, however, that very few people who do not give serious attention to achieving serious historical discourse in ordinary language actually do achieve it. Furthermore, it is my view that, within limits, the skills required for such discourse can be taught, and by some historians actually are being taught. I really am afraid that as an effect of *hubris* engendered by an overintensive diversion of time and energy into quantification, mathematization, and computerization, this fundamental historical skill will cease to receive such small attention as it now gets, which is far less attention than it actually needs. Indeed, I would go a little further and say that, of all historians, those now engaging in large-scale quantification stand in greatest need of having the indispensability of clarity and skill in historical writing brought to their attention.

Yours sincerely,
Jack

5 AYDELOTTE TO HEXTER, 24 FEBRUARY 1970

Department of History
University of Iowa
Iowa City, Iowa

Dear Jack:

Thank you for your fine letter. I am most grateful to you for allowing me to publish this correspondence, and also for the addition you have just made to it. When we discussed on the telephone the possibility of your writing this further letter I told you that I welcomed it enthusiastically and that my only stipulation was that I should be allowed equal time. I shall want at least that, since I have several comments. Though your case is admirably argued there are a number of points that cannot, in my judgment, be left quite as you put them.

You appear to have two general concerns, closely related but perhaps distinguishable: that the aptitude for expressing oneself in clear ordinary prose, which you regard as an indispensable tool of historical writing, is being obliterated by the development of quantification; and that historians who have gone in for quantitative methods have tended toward a one-sided approach, a single-minded commitment to these techniques that excludes other intellectual methods and tools. I know that you have been bothered about both these matters for some time. On both points I think we probably agree on general principles but may disagree as to how far quantification necessarily entails the unfortunate effects you ascribe to it and on how far it has in fact had these effects.

On the first questions you don't, of course, say that bad writing and slipshod thinking are attributable solely to the use of quantitative methods, and would agree that they have been produced often enough in the past without the aid of these elaborate technical contrivances. Nor, I think, would you insist that resort to quantification necessarily and inevitably entails the loss of the ability to write or think clearly. You do, nevertheless, seem to feel that there is a close connection between the two, and you identify loss of control of the language as a principal hazard in this type of research.

I grant the existence of the danger. Though I have not made a formal study—and I take it you have not either—comparing the prose styles of rigorously selected samples of quantifiers and nonquantifiers, it would be idle to deny the possibility of trouble on this front. It is only too easy for those who are unwary or uncritical to use a technique, particularly one that seems so promising, as an escape, an alternative route to self-satisfaction, which will serve to cover up their unwillingness or their inability to do hard thinking. Writing is a difficult skill to learn; students seldom write well to begin with; and a change in graduate education from an emphasis on writing papers to an emphasis on acquiring skills for the manipulation of data might well involve a substantial intellectual loss. This, by the way, is a problem for others beside historians. Some of my friends in other departments where quantitative methods are extensively used have expressed to me the concern that, in their fields, these methods may have been pushed too far or employed too exclusively, and that a new generation of graduate students may be appearing who tend to be technicians rather than thinkers. If anything like this is going on in history I should much regret it, and I am certainly continuing to place plenty of emphasis on intelligible writing in the training of my own students.

There is, however, another side to this question to which I don't think you do anything like justice. To take a basic point first, the incidental use of technical methods, far from obviating the need for careful and clear writing, makes it all the more urgent. As to the need for the continued use of the English language by historians, including quantifiers, with such effectiveness as they can muster, there can be no disagreement. Arithmetic is a bare language, incomparable in the special things it can do, but restricted. Whoever told you he hoped prose would soon be replaced by figures was, if he meant it seriously, certainly not expressing my position nor, I believe, the position of most of those who are knowledgeable about this kind of research. On the contrary, the plea for replacing words by numbers is based on a naive misunderstanding of what the quantitative approach is all about. This approach is nothing more than a convenient arrangement of some of the evidence for certain specific purposes. The figures do not, however, except on an elementary level, speak for themselves. Even after they have been assembled, the most challenging task still remains ahead: that of interpreting the evidence, making clear the problems to which it relates and what light it throws on them. This task is intellectual and not mechanical: it is performed not by solving an equation but by producing a convincing argument. Abandoning prose for figures not only does not represent the best practice; it represents a forlorn hope. Quantitative research, if it moves in this direction, is not likely to get far. All of this is, I think, fairly well recognized by the more accomplished of those who work with these methods.

It might be argued, and perhaps this is the line you would push, that, even if good writing is desirable for presentation of the results of quantitative research, such research has in fact produced a substantial amount of bad writing. However, the relation between cause and effect may not be that simple. Certainly I would not attempt to defend the literary style of some of the quantitative presentations I have seen. Yet I am not persuaded that their deficiencies necessarily result from the use of numbers. Is it not possible that bad writing and unclear thinking in such cases are to be attributed, not to the possession of new skills, but rather to the usual sources of these phenomena: carelessness and a lack of talent that would make themselves manifest in any field of endeavor? If you don't like the way some of these quantifiers are writing now, I cannot help wishing that you had had a chance to look at their efforts before they began to quantify; and I wonder whether their literary styles, even then, would have met your standards. The proposition of an inverse relationship between skill in the use of figures and skill in the use of words, in the sense that those good at one are likely to be bad at the other, might be hard to demonstrate. Bad writing and unclear thinking are hazards in all research; it would take a good deal to show that these hazards are necessarily greater in quantitative research than elsewhere. Furthermore, there are cases on the other side: a number of scholars have used highly technical methods of analysis and yet have been able to formulate their inferences and conclusions with lucidity and elegance. I like to think that they represent what is feasible along these lines and what we hope the best practice will come to be.

That is the negative side of the argument. The positive side is that a persuasive case can be made that systematic research, far from being an obstacle to clear thought, may actually be of some assistance. Your argument disregards or passes over what has been a principal gain in this kind of work, the sharpening of focus and the clarification of issues on which discussion had been confused or at cross purposes. As you yourself have said elsewhere, for historical problems that hinge on the question "how many?" the substitution of a number for an adjective is an intellectual improvement. It is also, I would add, a stylistic improvement. If I can judge from my own experience and that of my students, the use of arithmetic can contribute a good deal toward a more effective presentation. It is not the whole of the art of writing by any means, and what may properly be inferred from the data is always a matter of argument and not of mathematics. Yet the attempt to put a problem into a form in which it can be tested enforces a more precise formulation of it while, in the later stages of the research, getting one's data into intelligible order is an excellent preliminary step for clarifying one's thinking about them. A systematic review of the evidence can in this manner make a contribution to good writing, not by the criterion of rich, beautiful prose—confusion of thought may hide behind elegant rhetoric—but by the criterion of precise, careful, intelligible discourse in which proper attention is paid to the assumptions and implications of the argument. I wonder whether your admonitions may not be addressed to the wrong party. Doubtless everybody needs to be cautioned against carelessness, and we could all stand a little jacking up. It might be, however, that those who have not done systematic research are actually the ones who stand in greatest danger of writing unsatisfactory prose and of producing unclear, intellectually vulnerable statements.

As to your other main argument, the danger of a one-sided commitment to quantitative methods that excludes other techniques and approaches, I am once again in full agreement with you on general principles. Here, as before, your cautions are proper and well advised, and your letter calls attention in salutary fashion to the kinds of excesses that need to be avoided. People sometimes go hog-wild with these methods, use them for purposes for which they are not appropriate, and become so fascinated with the techniques that they acquire a false sense of security and forget or ignore important features of the problems they are trying to solve. There is always the danger that the undiscriminating will run a single approach into the ground; and we have had our share of individuals who overplay the mechanical aids and neglect the intellectual purposes they can be used to serve. Papers that consist mostly of tables, with a little bad English in between, are occasionally published. Not all ventures into quantitative history have been uniformly successful. Certainly a commitment to statistics to the exclusion of everything else can be limiting and barren; and I have been distressed by the intellectual poverty of some of the quantitative efforts I have seen.

Nevertheless, I cannot quite accept your version of the present state of quantitative research in history. You manage to leave the reader with the impression that a segment of the historical profession is on the brink, or slightly over the brink, of a disastrous new departure: that a group of obsessed fanatics who have no balance of judgment and no common sense, and are already well on the road to illiteracy, are swinging into a new kind of research in which all paths to knowledge except that through figures will be ignored.

I have no doubt that you could find some horrible examples to support your contentions. As a description of the situation as a whole, however, your view seems to me one-sided, and I think you are fastening a caricature derived from a limited number of extreme cases, a lunatic fringe, upon a large and reasonably reputable part of the profession. Excesses of the kind I have just been describing are, I assure you, deplored as much by those in the business as by bystanders like yourself. Though stupid papers are sometimes printed, in this line as in others, they do not win wide respect; and such papers may be objected to, or may be rejected for publication, for reasons that have nothing to do with the quality of the mathematics they contain. No one but a fool believes that measurement can be adopted as the sole tool of research.

What about the one example you cite, Lawrence Stone, on whose paper you were asked to comment and whose work you admire? You indicate that his success may be attributed to a divergence of practice from principle: to the fact that he has been faithless to his stated commitment to quantitative and systematic methods, and has used other approaches as well when they suited his purposes. All historians, however, who have made effective use of these techniques have been faithless to them in this sense. Actually, the analogy is false. The arrangement of evidence in tables is not an alternative path to salvation, automatically excluding all others. It is merely an incidental device that may sometimes help with part of the work. An exclusive commitment to it would be absurd. One might as well pledge undivided allegiance to the library catalogue, to the typewriter, or to the alphabet. These are all helpful, to be sure, but one uses other things as well, and a loyalty to one that excluded the others would be self-defeating. The notion that statisticians use only their figures and not their reasoning powers is a stereotype, a piece of folklore. Far from this, it is a cardinal precept in such work that the human mind must evaluate what is going on at every stage of the process. The kind of exclusiveness you deprecate is entirely contrary to good practice. You have no monopoly on loose-minded eclecticism.

I agree with you, of course, that quantification is not necessarily to be equated with merit, that it is not the only path to knowledge, and that no general rule can be laid down to the effect that all subjects are the better for being more quantified and the worse for being less quantified. On the contrary, the amount of further quantification needed in any given research situation depends on circumstances. It is a matter to be discussed, argued, and worked out in the light of the existing conditions and problems. There are some matters on which quantification can offer little or no assistance.

Granting all this, however, I still don't see that a modest increase in the use of quantitative techniques in history would pose a threat to the delicate methodological balance of the discipline. Nor do I believe that historians are likely to find themselves "muscle-bound" in a quantitative sense in the immediately forseeable future. Growing pains they may have but not, if I know the profession, a restricted mobility resulting from an overdeveloped mastery of this one technique. On the contrary, things are decidedly the other way round. The record of historical scholarship is full of missed opportunities: cases where a little intelligent counting could have helped materially but was, for some reason, never attempted. There are still lots of subjects on which quantitative or systematically organized information could be obtained, and on which it would be most useful to have it, and is high time that somebody did something about it. A one-sided, obsessed approach is something we would both regret, but a rectification of the balance is to be desired. I think a plausible case could be made that, at the moment, this rectification should be in the direction of more quantification rather than less. There is good reason to suppose that this tool, if used intelligently and with proper safeguards, can be a useful and promising one for further research.

The point could be put more strongly. The things you object to, unclear and careless exposition and a one-sided commitment to a single method, are exactly the sins that an experienced statistician wouldn't commit. As I indicated in one of my articles, these are standard traps against which beginners are regularly warned. The fact that some historians have fallen into them indicates how pitifully superficial their use of these methods has often been. The effectual remedy for the evils of which you complain is not less statistics but more: a more thorough grounding in the essentials of the subject and a more adequate understanding of its limitations as well as of its possibilities.

I come now to your demand for the production of the omelet. You mean, as the context indicates, to inquire what compensation the quantifiers can make or are prepared to make for the sacrifice of clear thinking and clear writing that seems to be entailed in their work. I do not, of course, agree that this sacrifice is necessary; indeed I hold that, if it is made, the outlook for quantitative research is poor and that efforts along this line might as well be abandoned. Also I don't agree that, in the best work, this sacrifice has been made. You manage to suggest, however, that the quantifiers owe a debt to the profession for the damage they have inflicted upon it, and that you would like to see some evidence that this debt has been or is going to be paid. The implication of this part of your letter is that the work of historians using quantitative techniques has been unimpressive. I don't know how far you would want to press this, since you have some pleasant things to say about quantitative research in your article in the *Journal of Contemporary History*. Yet the effect of your letter is to leave the reader, particularly a reader who hasn't read your article, with the impression that you regard the achievements of historians along this line, so far, as inconsiderable or useless, and that you have serious doubts about the profitability of the whole enterprise.

If this is your appraisal, I don't think it is a fair one. I am not sure what you mean by an omelet, but if you use the term as a symbol for sudden and dramatic solutions of a set of major problems, it can only be replied that the quantitative innovation is not of that character and that quantitative methods, like most other methods, don't work that way. The function of these techniques, as I have argued repeatedly, is a modest one, ancillary to the main tasks of research. It is merely to rearrange some of the evidence in a form in which its gist and general upshot can be more quickly ascertained. What one gets from doing this is not a dazzling revelation but a more convenient disposal of sections of the materials that may make possible some advance in the discussion of certain problems, in the hesitant, groping, stumbling way in which intellectual progress is ordinarily achieved.

Yet even these humble services can be useful. They permit historians to venture upon generalizations, and to test and examine them, in ways that would otherwise not be possible. The finding that an old generalization is not confirmed by the relevant evidence that can be assembled may, if placed in a proper intellectual context, constitute a significant step forward. Again, it can be useful to ascertain how much support can be found for each side of a contested argument. I have in my quantification article dealt with some of the other applications of these methods, and given a few illustrations.

Whether historians have taken intelligent advantage of these opportunities is another question. Your ire was apparently particularly aroused by some of the papers presented in Chicago. Possibly exception could be taken to a few of them; this is generally the case with papers delivered at any learned meeting. I happen to think that a number of them weren't all that bad but were, on the contrary, thoughtful, closely argued, and quite intelligible. The matter is too serious, however, to be decided by a verdict on a set of papers none of which have yet been published and a number of which were still in fairly rough form when we heard them presented. Any judgment on quantitative work as a whole would have to take into account other research such as, for example, that which I summarized in my *AHR* article, or the pieces that have been collected in several interesting recent anthologies. The value of these enterprises is, no doubt, a matter for argument, and the argument may not be settled until later, when we have more perspective. A number of these efforts, perhaps all of them, may be imperfect and incomplete. Yet it may already be possible to discern, in the best of them, a certain progress. If there has been little in the way of sudden revelations, which don't come all that often in history anyway, there has at least been a series of careful and responsible efforts to increase our understanding of certain problems by the use of research tools and of classes of information that had hitherto been inadequately exploited and that proved to have something of value to add. I think some of these efforts have made useful contributions and cannot properly be described as trivial or futile, and I should be sorry to see them cursorily dismissed in a formula that does not adequately reflect what they have to offer.

Yours sincerely,
Bill

6 HEXTER TO AYDELOTTE, 6 MARCH 1970

Department of History
Yale University
New Haven, Conn.

Dear Bill:

Thanks for your long and thoughtful letter. We always do come back to the same place. We are eye to eye on matters of principle, but make very different estimates of the actual situation to which the principles are supposed to apply. I nevertheless feel that there is some use in stating the principles over and over again. Perhaps a similar feeling accounts for the flood of dreary literature on the perfect prince in the fifteenth and sixteenth centuries. I do hope our efforts will not be quite as futile as those.

Very best regards,
Jack

LIST OF ARTICLES AND PAPERS BY THE AUTHOR PRESENTING SOME OF THE SUBSTANTIVE RESULTS OF HIS RESEARCH

1. "The House of Commons in the 1840's," *History* (new series), **XXXIX**, 137 (October 1954), pp. 249–262.

2. "Patterns of National Development: Introduction," in Philip Appleman, William A. Madden, and Michael Wolff, eds., *1859: Entering An age of Crisis* (Bloomington, Indiana, 1959), pp. 115–130.

3. "The Business Interests of the Gentry in the Parliament of 1841–47," published as an appendix to G. Kitson Clark, *The Making of Victorian England* . . . (London, 1962), pp. 290–305.

4. "Voting Patterns in the British House of Commons in the 1840s," *Comparative Studies in Society and History*, **V**, 2 (January 1963), pp. 134–163.

5. "Parties and Issues in Early Victorian England," *Journal of British Studies*, **V**, 2 (May 1966), pp. 95–114.

6. "The Country Gentlemen and the Repeal of the Corn Laws," *English Historical Review*, **LXXXII**, CCXXII (January 1967), pp. 47–60.

7. "The Conservative and Radical Interpretations of Early Victorian Social Legislation," *Victorian Studies*, **XI**, 2 (December 1967), pp. 225–236.

8. "Laissez-Faire and State Intervention in Mid-Nineteenth Century Britain," delivered at conference at Cornell University, 1967.

9. "The Disintegration of the Conservative Party in the Eighteen Forties: A Study of Political Attitudes," delivered at conference sponsored by Mathematical Social Science Board, University of Chicago, June 1969; and subsequently at annual meeting of the American Political Science Association, September 1969. Will be published in an anthology edicted by Robert W. Fogel, Allan G. Bogue, and the author.

ABCDE7987654321